WHEN YOUR SOULMATE IS - YOU

A Guide to Falling in Love With Who You Are

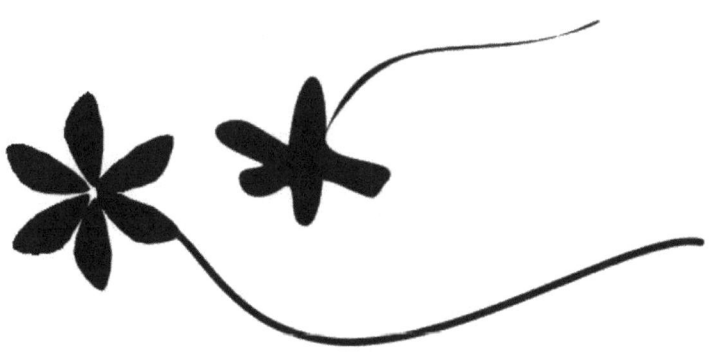

D. M. Woodard

Absolute Author
Publishing House

When Your Soulmate is – You
Copyright © 2020 by D. M. Woodard
All Rights Reserved.

All rights reserved. No part of this publication may be reproduced, distributed, or transmitted in any form or by any means, including photocopying, recording, or other electronic or mechanical methods, without the prior written permission of the AUTHOR, except in the case of brief quotations embodied in critical reviews and certain other noncommercial uses permitted by copyright law.

Although the author and publisher have made every effort to ensure that the information in this book was correct at press time, the author and publisher do not assume and hereby disclaim any liability to any party for any loss, damage, or disruption caused by errors or omissions, whether such errors or omissions result from negligence, accident, or any other cause. This book is not intended as a substitute for the medical advice of physicians. The reader should regularly consult a physician in matters relating to his/her health and particularly with respect to any symptoms that may require diagnosis or medical attention.

Publisher: Absolute Author Publishing House
Editor: Mypurplepen @Fiverr
Interior Designer: Dr. Melissa Caudle
Cover Designer: Rebeca @Rebecacovers

Library of Congress Catalogue In-Publication-Data

When Your Soulmate is – You/D. M. Woodard

    p. cm.

ISBN: 978-1-64953-031-8

    1.   Self-help 2. Women's Literature 2. Spirituality

Nature lover and a conservation contributor to land in Glencoe and Lochabar, Scotland.

DEDICATION

This book is a product of what one feels for self, the delicate act of finding love within oneself and accepting all that hits one. It comes with a subconscious attribute to life, love, feeling, and an outpouring of genuine emotions. However, this piece of work is exclusively a product and a fusion of my children's support, Jonica and Shenay for their acceptance and love.

I, _____

(YOUR NAME)

hereby promise and affirm that I will read the entire book, cover to cover. This will plant the seed in my mind that will assist in my personal growth and allow me to accept that my soulmate is in the reflection of my mirror.

TABLE OF CONTENTS

INTRODUCTION	i
Be Your Own Champion!	iv
Look After Yourself	iv
CHAPTER ONE	1
LOVING YOURSELF	1
Ways To Fall (And Stay) In Love With Yourself	1
CHAPTER TWO	15
LAW OF ATTRACTION	15
Law of Vibration	16
What are the 7 Laws of Attraction?	19
How Do You Manifest What You Want?	20
How And Why Does The Law Of Attraction Work?	21
Your Relationship To The Universe	21
How To Use The Law Of Attraction (And What For)?	25
Your Intentions Vs Other People's Intentions	26
Why Persistence Is The Key To The Law Of Attraction	34
Exercises That Help You Attract What You Desire	35
CHAPTER THREE	41
THE ART OF SELF-HELP	41
New Way Of Life With Self-Help	44
Where To Make The Change	45

CHAPTER FOUR	50
SELF-CARE TIPS	50
Why is self-care so important?	51
Why is self-control important?	55
How do you take care of yourself emotionally?	56
What role does self-care play in mental health?	56
Self-Help Tips That Will Take You to the Next Level	57
CHAPTER FIVE	65
BUILD UP YOUR SELF-ESTEEM	65
Healthy Self-esteem	70
Steps to an Improved Self-Esteem	75
CHAPTER SIX	79
YOU OWE YOURSELF AN APOLOGY	79
How to Apologize Appropriately	81
CHAPTER SEVEN	84
DEFEATING THE ENEMY INSIDE OF YOU	84
Two sides of the same coin	89
Steps to accepting your perceived self	89
The cycle of change	90
The way others see you	91
CHAPTER EIGHT	92
AVOID LOSING YOUR CORE IDENTITY	92
What's Your Identity?	92
"Me" Becomes "We"	93
How To Get Yourself Back	94
CHAPTER NINE	98

YOU ARE YOUR SOULMATE	98
What if soulmate manifestation was easy?	98
Forgiveness: The Critical Law of Attraction Step	101
Break the cycle!	102
CONCLUSION	104
ABOUT THE AUTHOR	107

INTRODUCTION

Now, nothing is complete without delving within your psyche and therein lays the secrets of your life, your heart, and your absolute truth to identity, your exquisite character traits. It is quite easy to commence and all you have to do is choose some nice instrumental music like a Chopin Nocturne.

Keeping the volume down low, just lay on your couch and allow your mind to quieten, while exhaling deeply and inhaling slowly and deeply. Repeat this breathing exercise for a wee while and then just relax and allow your body and mind to come still.

You may find that with the aid of certain stimulants like beta waves your meditation experiences shall be richer and more invigorating. This is something you can experiment with as you become familiar with the pleasure of relaxation and feel your energy increasing. Prayer is an attractive addition to all forms of reflection and actually during meditation allows your inner voice to communicate with The Almighty on a spiritual level.

The most beneficial thing to do next is plan an exercise program to tie in with your discovery and expedition through the real you. Avoid soft drinks like the plague and minimize alcohol and desserts like chocolate, cookies, and sweets in order to compliment the new essence of the revelation of you. There is nothing more damaging to the soul than overindulgence in any endeavor, so practice moderation and soon it will be as spontaneous as breathing.

With a pen and paper write down three things you are grateful for, and then meditate on their relevance in your life. Gratitude is the amazing surprising link toward lifting our spirits and assuring us that we make a difference in this world.

Say a wee prayer and if you cannot think of any prayers, well just make something up in conversation mode. All The Almighty requires of us is to chat with him like you would with any friend over the phone or even in person.

Humor is the lift your psyche calls out for and the lighter our heart is with good cheer the better we shall feel no matter the situation. Sing if you like to, even if you do not have a good voice, just go ahead and sing in the shower or while doing housework, as this releases an incredible amount of negative energy which holds the potential to heal from within. It also helps to clear out your lungs inviting fresh air into them with each cleansing breath. Speaking of air, make trips to the park, or if you live in the country, make plans to take walks or hikes.

Please know that all changes have to commence within, so take your time and become familiar with the things that were distracting you from experiencing self-love in the first place. As they pop into your mind, analyze them deleting them as necessary or implementing the required instructions you may receive to quell their persistent annoyance.

It is easier than you think and takes a bit of daily practice and in no time at all your aura will be one of magical calm exuding harmony and attractiveness. The majority of the time we never actually become acquainted with ourselves until maybe some disaster comes along and we are confined to bed or within the parameters of our home.

There are three amazing but simple beliefs one may implement to reinforce self-love. The first is to know the Almighty loves you and he desires that you embrace him as he has an abundance of unconditional love for you. Say a prayer of thanks to him in advance as you seek his guidance through your journey.

Secondly, no matter what you may think there are people in your life who also love you and if you stop and look you will notice the little things they do for you. Offer your supportive friends and family some gratitude too, as there is nothing like gratitude to attract good tidings.

Thirdly, the fact that you are on this journey spells it out quite clearly that you have a certain amount of self-love already in place and that is an excellent foundation on which to build. Look in the mirror and tell yourself that with each day your self-love shall increase, as will your health, strength, and wealth.

Commence on an expedition to develop your home into a studio dedicated to enhance your attractiveness. First off, get rid of all unnecessary clutter in your home and surrounds, everything that you do not need. In fact, if this is something you find difficult to do, then seek the assistance of a friend. Play nice upbeat music as often as you can and avoid too much exposure to the daily news and other news channels.

One particular area to clear out of all clutter is your bedroom and closet as there must be clothes you have not worn in ages but definitely longer than a year. Fill as many bags as you can and drop them off to the St. Vincent DePaul Society, or similar agency in your area that recycles second hand clothes. Make sure you do not sell them but give them away as this has beneficial agents for stimulating benevolence.

Now that you have begun this, take it to the next step and coordinate your clothes and shoes in systematic arrangements. If your room could do with some fresh paint choose a nice calm colour and perhaps make some other changes like bed coverings and window dressings. Adding some nice pictures on the walls and perhaps a couple of plants too as these will freshen the air, which will benefit you as you sleep.

As you wander through your home, make notes mentally or written about other things you could effect as changes over a period of time as not everything has to be done immediately. In fact, if you synchronize the changes with your mindset it shall be more rewarding as your improved self-love may desire different accents than you have currently, so limit completing everything all at once.

It is thought that the most important relationship you will ever have is the one with yourself. This rings true for me. If you feel good about yourself then the chances are that this will be reflected back to you in your relationships with others.

Loving yourself means accepting yourself as you are; faults and all. You may wish to work towards self-improvement AND still love yourself in the process. It's about letting go of all the judgments and criticisms of yourself and treating yourself as you would your best friend. It's about having a healthy regard and self-respect for yourself and appreciating all of your wonderful qualities.

Here are some tips for nurturing and loving yourself:

Be Your Own Champion!

You are unique, there is no one else quite like you in the world and for that you are a treasure and a gift to the world. Stand up for yourself, cheer yourself on, give yourself a pat on the back when you've done well and treat yourself with compassion if you make a mistake.

Look After Yourself

Many people in our society are driven to work long hours, neglecting their health and their fitness. As a result their relationships and health suffer and stress levels rocket.

Good self-care is the foundation stone of a rich and fulfilling life. Self-care includes adequate rest and time doing things that bring you joy and energy, and having a balance between work and personal life. Practicing self-care can make you feel you are being selfish. But taking care of your precious self is important for your present and future well-being. It also means you are in a better position to be there for others. One analogy is the flight attendant telling adult passengers to put oxygen masks on themselves before their babies in case of emergency, in order to be breathing well enough to care for their children.

Take Yourself On A Date

Enjoy spending time with yourself. Set aside some time within the next fortnight to spend a few hours with yourself doing things that you love. It could be anything - going to see a film, taking a walk, listening to music, taking yourself out for a lovely meal. Treat yourself as you would a precious loved one.

CHAPTER ONE

LOVING YOURSELF

There's little time left over on hectic days. You're stretched thin tying your kid's shoelaces, remembering to bring in treats for your co-worker's birthday, and volunteering to join another committee. But if it's been awhile since you did something nice for yourself, it's time to prioritize some self-love!

Self-love influences everything from who you date, to how you are perceived at work, to how well you cope when the kids test your limits at home. It's beneficial to your mental health, so there's no need to feel guilty about taking some time for yourself. Plan to give some time, attention, and affection to the most important person in your life. Indulge in some serious self-care and get to know yourself even better. Here are nine creative ideas for how to get started.

Ways To Fall (And Stay) In Love With Yourself

Just like any relationship, we have to fight to keep the connection we have with ourselves healthy and thriving. If you're feeling disillusioned with yourself, here are 40 simple ways you can kick your relationship back into high gear – and keep it there come hell or high water.

1. Master a routine that works for you.

Figure out if you're an early bird or a night owl; a schedule-oriented person or a play-it-by-ear person, and then set up a routine that works for you. If you aren't able to keep yourself grounded in a lifestyle that facilitates growth, you're going to have a hard time keeping your self-concept stable.

2. Maintain a (mostly) healthy diet.

As much as we'd like to believe that our diets don't affect the way we're feeling and thinking, we'd be sorely mistaken in that claim. Our physical health has a massive impact on our day-to-day sense of wellbeing and putting the right foods into our body can make a world of difference when it comes to how we feel about ourselves.

3. Find a form of exercise you love.

You don't have to run a marathon or tackle Mount Everest. But the sooner you find a form of exercise that you genuinely enjoy taking part in, the greater an appreciation for your own body you will develop. And when you're at peace inside your body, it's infinitely easier to be at peace inside your mind.

4. Travel once a year.

Keep your relationship with yourself fresh by taking it on the road at least once a year. Travel somewhere that forces you out of your routine or comfort zone. You will be forced to develop in new ways and will consequently make some great memories.

5. Read a new book every month.

Don't allow your thought patterns to become lazy and repetitive. Once a month, read something that challenges your way of thinking and gives your mind something new and interesting to turn over.

6. Be vulnerable with friends and loved ones.

Open yourself up to the people who love and support you. It takes true strength to share yourself with others, but that closeness is something we all need.

7. Forgive yourself for your mistakes.

Take the time to understand your past thought patterns and forgive yourself for the poor actions they lead to. Without understanding we cannot make changes going forward. And the commitment to making those changes will be something that you're ultimately proud of.

8. Confront your own weaknesses and fears.

Once a year, pick a fear that you've been harbouring for too long and find a way to face it head on. You'll gain a greater sense of self-respect for having done so and you'll be down one fear to boot!

9. Maintain healthy relationships with family members.

A healthy relationship with yourself means the ability to maintain healthy relationships with others. Let friends, relatives and loved ones play an active role in your life. The more open you are to others, the more open you are to your life.

10. Listen to TED talks or inspirational speeches once a week.

As fantastic as it is to grow and be inspired by the experiences of people we know, it never hurts to listen to the experiences of those that are vastly different than ourselves, and those who've put a significant amount of energy into researching and sharing their knowledge of a particular field.

11. Make time to pursue new interests and hobbies.

Take that cooking class you've always wanted to take. Read up on that topic you've been wanting to explore. It's never too late to pick up on something new and fascinating, and you owe it to yourself to do so.

12. Allow yourself to be surprised by life.

Say 'Yes' to that event that you'd normally say 'No' to. Go out on a date with that cute stranger. Let plans bend in ways you wouldn't normally expect them to and be open to whatever comes next. To keep your relationship with yourself fresh, you have to keep your relationship with the world around you fresh too.

13. Check in with yourself once a week.

Keep a journal of your thoughts or check in with a close friend once a week to measure the progress you're making toward your goals and to keep in touch with your overall sense of wellbeing.

14. Learn how to prioritize money.

It's important to be aware of what a your financial priorities are. You owe it to yourself to splurge every once in a while, but in order to do that you have to figure out how you like to allocate your money and where you can make leniencies.

15. Reflect on what has made you the happiest in the past.

Until we understand where our happiest memories come from and why, it's going to be tricky to recreate those circumstances in the future.

16. Reflect on what's made you the unhappiest in the past.

Look for patterns in the circumstances and behaviors that have hindered your happiness historically. There's no sense in repeating old mistakes.

17. Learn how to say 'No' to yourself.

Learning to be strict with yourself is an integral component to self-love. You have to know what your top priorities are in life, and which passing fancies you may have to give up in order to move toward them.

18. Learn how to say 'No' to others.

Learn to turn down commitments you don't want to go to and favours that you don't want to run. Your time is important. Why waste it?

19. Keep a running list of long-term goals.

Keep in check with the goals and dreams that are burning inside of you; they're what will keep you going through every bump in the road.

20. Learn to take credit for your accomplishments.

Own what you've done, both in public and in private. Keep a running list of things you have done that you're proud of, that you can pull out when you need a little boost.

21. Force yourself to ask for what you want, even when it's uncomfortable.

Ask for that job. That promotion. That date. You'll feel better about yourself for having done so, even if the answer is no.

22. Make laughter a priority.

Watch a half-hour of stand-up comedy or phone your most hilarious friend once a week if not more. Make your abs ache for all the right reasons.

23. Look presentable more days than not.

No matter how little value you place on your physical appearance, the more presentable you look the more put-together you tend to feel. And the more put-together you feel, the more ready you are to face each day.

24. Challenge your own thoughts and beliefs by reading literature or talking to people who disagree with you.

Don't let yourself become so wrapped up in your own worldview that your thoughts become stagnant and tired. Chat with people who hold opposing viewpoints to your own or at the least read what they have to say. It never hurts to challenge your thinking.

25. Let your loved ones know how much you value them.

Don't let those important 'I love you's' go unsaid. You'll sleep easier each night knowing that the people you care about know exactly how you feel.

26. Find an activity that is affirming for you and practice it daily.

Find something that capitalizes on your strengths, be it exercising, gardening, reading, performing or socializing, and make a routine out of it. Who says you can't have a little pick-me-up every day?

27. Invest in something bigger than yourself.

It can be a religion, a charity or even just a social group that meets once a week. It feels good to be a part of something bigger than yourself, no matter how big or small an influence you have.

28. Spend at least half an hour outside every day.

Sunlight is a natural mood enhancer. The more time you're spending outdoors, the more at peace you're going to feel with yourself.

29. Make getting eight hours of sleep every night a priority.

Getting an adequate amount of sleep can absolutely make or break a day – and when you're consistently under-rested you're consistently at odds with yourself.

30. Have an orgasm at least twice a week.

Have it alone or with company, give yourself that physical release. You'll quickly go crazy without it.

31. Make music a regular part of your routine.

Find out which kind of music pumps you up, which mellows you out, and which kind you ought to play when.

32. Schedule alone time with yourself.

Make you-time an active priority. To keep up a relationship you have to invest quality time and that includes your relationship with yourself.

33. Recognize what you need help with (and can outsource).

If a biweekly cleaning service will take a load off your plate, make a financial plan that will account for it. Knowing your natural weaknesses are the first step in combatting them.

34. Strategically indulge your desires.

Learn to recognize when you need a break, and then indulge that need in whichever way suits you best.

35. Unplug for one full day each month.

For at least twelve straight hours a month, turn off all of your electronics and immerse yourself in the world around you. You may be surprised what you find.

36. Take care of your physical environment.

Keep your home, office and other living spaces maintained in a fashion that makes you feel at peace. You'll thank yourself for keeping your headspace clear.

37. Welcome external feedback.

Check in with friends, family and loved ones regularly to ask them how they think you are doing. Let them be honest and take their feedback to heart.

38. Make peace with what you're never going to make a priority.

You may never be the world's most athletic person or a New York Bestselling author. And sometimes, simply acknowledging that you're choosing not to make something a priority goes a long way in reducing your stress level around it.

39. Give yourself credit where credit is due.

Don't explain away or downplay your accomplishments. Take pride in how far you have come and how much you've accomplished for yourself.

40. Allow your relationship with yourself to constantly and intentionally evolve.

Just as we have to let our relationships with others fluctuate, alter and grow, we have to let our relationships with ourselves do the same. After all, you've got the rest of your life to spend with yourself. So, you might as well make it a relationship worth being in.

YOU FIRST

To be loved is a wonderful thing. However, you must first love yourself. There is no way that you can receive love the way it is intended to be given if you do not love yourself. Loving yourself means taking care of your body, inside and out. It is a task to stay healthy with all of the temptation that is out there. In order to conquer this task we must really look at why we are doing it.

Some of us indulge in unhealthy habits because it makes us feel good and others overindulge because there is a deep rooted issue within us that needs to be addressed. A lot of these deep rooted issues arise from our childhood experiences. We do not realize how easily children are affected and influenced by the actions of others in early childhood. These events can rear their ugly head later on in adulthood through many different unhealthy activities. Now that we are adults it is up to us to evaluate ourselves in an effort to find that link. This may very painful and difficult, but it will be worth it. Once you have pinpointed the causes of your actions you can begin the journey of repairing yourself and making a better life for you and those you come in contact with. During this process you will have to face the dimensions of yourself that you may not be that fond of but doing so will help you appreciate your entire existence.

Find meaning in those areas that you look upon as negative, because the more you fight against them and bury them deep inside the more issues you will continue to have. Yes, you may say, leave well enough alone, because things seem to be working out well. However, at some point something will happen that will be a trigger and all these feelings and characteristics that you felt were not good or beneficial will be dredged up and it will be devastating to your entire being. Therefore, it is better to deal with the whole self on your terms. What I mean by on your terms is you can decide when you want to explore your entire being and how long you want to take. It will not be as a result of something triggering you. You will be making a conscious effort to get to know and love the entire existence of yourself.

You will find that once you have begun this process life will be easier to live. You will still have challenges, heartache, and pain, but you will be better equipped to handle it and you will find positive in the experience instead of negative. During this process you may want to employ the help of a therapist, which will guide and support you through the process. Please, get over the misconception that therapists are only for those who have severe mental issues. Therapists are very successful in making mentally healthy people even more mentally healthy. Therefore, if this process begins to be overwhelming, seek professional help.

The journey of loving yourself is not easy, but it is well worth it. You no longer portray to have confidence, self-esteem, and love for yourself. Instead, you will possess these attributes and because of the hard work that went into obtaining them, it will be very difficult for them to be taken away.

When you love yourself, you receive more love in return. When you exude confidence and joy, you'll attract others with the same zest for living. This improves the quality of your relationships, which improves your life. The cycle is clear, and it all starts with falling in love with yourself. But where does self-love come from? And how can you build it? What are the best ways to fall in love with yourself?

1. Be kind to yourself

It seems simple, but it can be one of the hardest acts of self-love to master. We grow up in a society that is always telling us how to look, how to live, and even how to feel. If you're wondering how to fall in love with yourself, the first step is to give yourself permission to be human. You don't have to be a super-mom, a fitness model or a billionaire to be worthy of love.

2. Change your self-talk

"Beliefs have the power to create and the power to destroy," says Tony Robbins, motivational speaker. The way you talk to yourself affects your mood and your behavior, and negative inner thoughts become a self-fulfilling prophecy. It's okay to hold yourself to high standards and to feel negative emotions occasionally, but don't get stuck in a cycle of negativity. Catch yourself when you fall into negative self-talk and make a conscious effort to change your words into something positive.

Change your self-talk incantation.

3. Adjust your physical state

Your physical state, which is your posture, breath, and movement, is the key to your emotional state. If you're not feeling confident, try adjusting your body. Straighten your spine and throw your shoulders back. Raise your head high. Smile. Get in a power pose, like standing with your head raised and your arms in a "V" shape or crossed behind your head. These actions send signals to your brain that you're proud and confident. And when you feel that way, it's easy to fall in love with yourself.

4. Meditate

Meditation is one way to not only change your breath, which is part of your physical state, but also to change your entire mindset. You can also try incantations, which are a vivid visualization of something you want, repeated with enthusiasm and belief. The phrase, "I am worthy of love," said with a smile and a confident posture can go a long way to manifesting love in your life. Visualizing your goals is another form of meditation that can reprogram your brain into a state of self-love.

5. Create healthy relationships

It's true that your most important relationship is with yourself, but that doesn't mean you should allow negativity into your life. Surround yourself with people who care about you and think the best of you. Use the cardinal rules of love to create healthy relationships that bring positivity to your life, and let go of any relationships that aren't supportive and caring. You won't just fall in love with yourself, you'll find your whole life improves.

6. Adopt an abundance mindset

When you practice gratitude and adopt an abundance mindset in everything you do, that will naturally bubble over into falling in love with yourself. Find the good in every situation, and stop reading too much into the negative. If you had a bad date, you might think, "I'll never find love." Neutralize that thought by thinking about all the love you already have from friends and family, and all the fun dates you've been on.

7. Go off the grid

Taking the time to relax, recharge, and reconnect with your core being can help you discover how to fall in love with yourself. If your brain is always on, you're living in a heightened, unsustainable state. Self-reflection can affirm our sense of ourselves and help us learn from our mistakes. Richard Branson, Chairman of the Virgin Group, has his best ideas when he disconnects from his smartphone for a couple of days at a time. Journalist and businessman, Tony Schwartz, credits disconnecting with rediscovering a deeper part of himself. Additionally, research on relaxation is clear -- giving your brain a break actually results in increased creativity and productivity, higher motivation, and a sharper memory.

8. Practice self-care

When you love yourself, you treat yourself kindly, both emotionally and physically. You wouldn't want a person you love to live in a stressed state of mind or to avoid doing things they love, so why allow yourself to do those things? Establishing habits of self-care, like eating healthy and exercising, can train your brain to think positively. The best way to fall in love with yourself is to create a life you love and surround yourself with people who love you. That makes loving yourself easy.

9. Have fun

Take the time to create joyful habits and do things that you love. Put on your favorite music and dance around the kitchen. Play a game with your kids or grandkids. Immerse yourself in a good book. Go for a hike and get out in nature. Give yourself a chance to get out of your own head, and you just might find you're falling in love with the new, spontaneous you.

10. Do something you're good at

Do you play an instrument, write short stories, or grow the best tomatoes in town? Doing something you're good at reinforces your confidence and shows you how to fall in love with yourself, by appreciating your own skills. If you can share them with others, that's even better. You just might find others enjoy your talents too.

11. Push yourself

Of course, if we do things we're good at, we'll never grow. It's essential to get out of your comfort zone and push your boundaries. Learn a new skill. Take a public speaking course. Join a singles group. You'll see that you're stronger, more resilient and more capable than you thought possible, and that's how you really fall in love with yourself.

12. Take credit

Many of us are naturally modest. We're often team-oriented and underplay our own accomplishments in the name of keeping harmony. But taking credit can be good for your self-esteem, and that can help you fall in love with yourself. If your neighbor compliments your piano-playing skills or your friends notice your new public speaking abilities, don't downplay it. Give them sincere thanks, and take it to heart. You deserve praise.

13. Find your purpose

Finding your purpose is the ultimate way to learn how to fall in love with yourself. Purpose gives us a reason to get up in the morning and makes us a part of something larger than ourselves. It fulfills several of our 6 Human Needs, including significance, growth, and contribution. But purpose rarely reaches out and knocks on our door. To find your purpose, you need to be honest with yourself. What are you most excited about in your life? What brings you joy? Once you uncover meaning in your life, you'll start to see the bigger picture, and stop criticizing the smaller things.

14. Give back

The secret to living is giving. Giving back is the ultimate purpose in life and is also the secret to falling in love with yourself. When you have a sense of purpose, you'll live confidently and stop looking for external affirmation. You know that you have intrinsic worth, because you have gifts to give the world. And when you truly believe that you are here for a reason, loving yourself comes naturally. Find your purpose and light a fire of self-love within you, and others will be attracted to the flames.

CHAPTER TWO

LAW OF ATTRACTION

Of all the universal laws, the law of attraction is both the most fascinating and the most misunderstood. Fascinating, because as humans we naturally want a tool to help create the life of our dreams, and the law of attraction can certainly help us to do that. Misunderstood because, unlike a tool that we can pull out and use now and again, but is otherwise inactive, the law of attraction is operating in our lives constantly and independently, whether we are consciously aware of it, or believe in it, or not.

In other words, there is no need to engage the law of attraction, it is already at work in your life and always will be. So long as you are alive and breathing, the law of attraction is at work. This is great news! You are already using the law of attraction to create everything in your life whether you realise it or not. The results that you are experiencing in your career, finances, relationships, health, home, community, and so on, are a direct result of the law of attraction and your interaction with it in the form of thoughts and feelings.

If you're not creating the kind of life you want though, chances are you are creating by default, allowing the law of attraction to bring you more and more of the same. Unfortunately, we weren't handed a life manual at birth and, for many of us, our parents were not aware of the law of attraction and so they did not teach us. In order to really understand the law of attraction, you first must understand another of the universal laws, the law of vibration.

Law of Vibration

According to the law of vibration, everything is made of energy and has a distinct frequency or vibration. With the advent of powerful technology, science now agrees. Quantum physicists have shown that, although matter may appear to be solid, when you look at it through a high-powered microscope so that it is broken down into its smallest components which includes molecules, atoms, neutrons, electrons and quanta (the smallest particles measurable); it is ultimately mostly empty space interspersed with energy.

In other words, at the quantum level, everything is comprised of energy and empty space and what makes you, your home, your car, the chair you're sitting in, seem solid is the frequency of the vibration of the energy that makes it up.

Your body and all that you consider to be "you" has a distinct and unique vibration (or more correctly a mix of vibrations). Your creations, in the form of thoughts, also have distinct vibrations that affect or blend with your overall vibration.

In turn, your vibrations affect everything around you, your environment, the people, and animals around you, the inanimate objects, even the seemingly 'empty' space and they, in turn, affect you. That's why, when you walk into a room where there was an earlier argument, you can sense it. We even use terms like "bad vibes," "you can feel the tension." and "you could cut the air in here with a knife," to describe it. In each case what we are referring to is the energy imprint of the earlier occupants.

Similarly, you may have gone to someone's home, office or business where, as soon as you entered, you felt the "good vibes" that filled the place. That's because, over time, a place becomes imbued with the energy imprints of the dominant vibrations of the people who live or work there. So a home, for example, can literally become filled with love or tension or anger or sadness or any other emotion, and that home will feel that way to a visitor even if none of the regular occupants are at home at the time. If you've ever entered such a place you may even have noticed how you just relaxed and felt good in response to the "good vibes" around you. Of course, the extent to which you take on the vibrations of the people and things around you is up to you, but for most people, this is not a conscious decision.

So, you are giving off vibrations every second of every day. You are also simultaneously receiving and translating the vibrations of everything and everyone around you. If we use the analogy of television, you are both a television transmitter, beaming out your own unique station, and also a television set or receiver, able to tune in to all the stations or frequencies being broadcast around you. Sometimes we refer to these incoming vibrations as intuition or "gut feelings."

So, how do you know what your vibration is at any moment?

Simple - ask yourself how you are feeling.

Your emotions are a quick and handy guide to your vibration in any moment. If you feel loving, you are vibrating at the frequency of love; if you feel angry, you are vibrating at the frequency of anger; if you feel curious, you are vibrating at the frequency of curiosity, and those vibrations are received by everything and everyone around you. You are also, through the law of attraction, bringing to you more experiences that will match this vibration so when you feel angry the law of attraction will bring to you more experiences that will elicit the feeling of anger, you will attract angry people and find yourself in the middle of angry situations.

Have you ever had a day where you felt lousy, but tried to pretend that everything was okay to family, friends, or co-workers? It doesn't work, does it? Your friends, family or co-workers know straight away that you are not how you are pretending to be. They may ask if something is wrong, or comment that you don't seem to be your normal self. They pick up on the incongruence between what you are saying and your vibration. Because we are not used to explaining in terms of vibrations, they may attribute their knowing to something more mundane like the tone of voice or body language. Still, even people without the full use of their senses can detect this type of incongruence.

To sum up, you are sending out vibrations every moment of every day. Those vibrations are a mix of your thoughts and feelings and they affect everything around you. At the same time, you are also receiving and translating the vibrations of everything around you, which can, in turn, affect your vibration by how you react to them. Now that we understand vibration, let's look at how it interacts with the law of attraction.

Law of Attraction

The law of attraction, simply put, means energy attracts energy. You may also have heard it expressed as "like attracts like," "that which is like unto itself is drawn," and even "thoughts become things."

The law of attraction is at work in your life every minute of every day. Your vibrations are constantly being broadcast to, and received, by the universe. This activates the law of attraction which then matches your vibrations and attracts to you similar vibrations in the form of people, things, and situations in your life. In other words, you are always creating your life through your thoughts and feelings. The conditions in your life, whether they are what you want or not, are always a match to your dominant vibrations.

The law of attraction, like all the universal laws, operates whether you are aware of it or not, or believe it or not. The often-used terms "what you focus on grows", "careful what you wish for (cause you just might get it)", "birds of a feather flock together" and "you can't get enough of what you don't want" are all examples of ways that we describe the law of attraction in action.

So, the question becomes - if your life is not how you would wish it to be, how do you change it? And the answer most often given by law of attraction and personal development teachers is a simple one - change your thoughts.

Simple - yes, but not easy. Here's why.

Somewhere between 94 - 98% of all thoughts are subconscious, that is, below or out of conscious awareness which means that only 2 - 6% of your thoughts are ever conscious. So, even if you managed to change all of your conscious thoughts to be positive, that still leaves an awful lot of subconscious thought, at least some of which would be negative, vibrating away in the background without you even being aware of it! If you're having trouble creating what you want in life, chances are your subconscious mind is at fault.

Believe it or not, the Law of Attraction isn't a complicated magic ritual that requires initiation into an ancient, mystery school or secret order.

In fact, the Law of Attraction is a simple and unchanging universal principle.

What are the 7 Laws of Attraction?

There are 7 laws of attraction. Use them well to achieve whatever you desire. These include:

1. Unwavering Desire

2. Conceptualization and Imagination

3. Affirmation

4. Focus with Confidence

5. Profound Belief

6. Gratitude

7. Manifestation

Think of the Law of Attraction as gravity.

Toss a penny from your roof, it lands on the ground. Try to jump off your couch, you'll hit the ground.

Gravity is an unchanging law of our universe. And understanding the law of gravity allows you to predict what will happen.

The Law of Attraction works the same way.

Things within our universe tend to migrate toward other like things. We're using the word "things" here, because this law encompasses thoughts, feelings, people, objects and everything else in our universe.

It's a universal principle, so it applies to all things.

Like migrates toward like.

Believing it's true or untrue doesn't change anything. It's a simple universal principle. However, the better you understand it, the more you can start predicting and expecting what happens to you, for you. Your awareness of the Law of Attraction can change your life.

How Do You Manifest What You Want?

There is a simple formula. First of all, you need to decide what you really want (or don't want).

Now you just need to ask the universe!

Well, how do I do that? Esay.

You are a part of that universe. Here are the steps you should take:

Work hard. Trust in your work. Receive the help and acknowledge it.

Your energetic vibrations are like radio signals. You must tune your signal to a vibration worthy of receiving it, meaning stay positive and thankful.

How And Why Does The Law Of Attraction Work?

Just as the "why" of the law of gravity is complex and difficult to understand (unless you are a theoretical physicist) the "why" of the Law of Attraction is also somewhat complicated.

Gravity is actually still a bit of a mystery to scientists. We understand that gravity prevents us and everything else on Earth from floating away, but the exact "why" is an intricate matter.

The Law of Attraction is similar. As with all the laws of our universe, we understand that these laws do work, even though we don't necessarily understand how to define them.

Knowing and thinking that you can do something will motivate you to do it.

It's like the old good "fake it 'til you make it."

So, how does the Law of Attraction work in this context?

If you think positive, you will get a positive outcome, and vice versa. It's basically synonymous with "you are what you think."

Your Relationship To The Universe

To really understand the Law of Attraction, tune in to your perception of your relationship with the universe. In other words, it's important to examine how you feel about the way the universe interacts with you.

Do you believe you can influence your surroundings so things happen for you? Or do you believe things happen TO you?

In psychology, this perspective is called, "Internal vs. External Locus of Control."

Some people believe that they are a product of everything that has happened to them. This is called an external locus of control, because these people believe they are not in control of their lives. The goal of therapy is for patients to realize that they actually have an internal locus of control.

The Law of Attraction works the same way.

The truth is, your thoughts and feelings do have an effect on the events that take place around you. A shift in your perspective and understanding of the truth about your relationship to the universe can begin to attract better things into your life.

It's Not Magic, It's Science

At this point, you may still remain unconvinced that this principle — like attracts like — is a scientific one. It may still seem interwoven in magic and, therefore, unreal.

Perhaps it's because we're talking about intangible concepts like thoughts and feelings. With gravity, an apple thrown up into the air falls onto the ground. You may not understand it, but you can visibly and immediately experience the effects.

It's difficult to imagine that thoughts and feelings can have an effect on the world around us. Fortunately, advances in technology and science allow us to visibly and immediately experience the effects of our thoughts. Just like watching an apple fall through the air, there are experiments that demonstrate the immediate effects of thoughts and feelings.

Believe it or not, there are volumes of scientific evidence to prove that our thoughts alone have immediate and tangible effects on ourselves and the environment around us.

Here Are Top Scientific Experiments And Studies That Prove It Right:

1. The Summer of '93 D.C. Meditation Experiment

A group of 4,000 people volunteered to meditate on peace and love to reduce the amount of crime in the high-crime Washington, DC area. A team of scientists and researchers approached the project without bias and tested for every variable imaginable.

The results were clear -- during the month of meditation, crime dropped by 25%, definitively and scientifically proving that the positive thoughts of a group of people can affect and change the behavior of ill-intentioned individuals.

2. Thinking You're Younger Physically Makes You Younger

In 1979, a study was conducted on 70-80-year-old men to see the difference between remembering youth fondly and actually reliving youth.

One group talked and reminisced about their younger days while the other group actually pretended to be young, surrounding themselves with TV shows, music and activities of their youth.

At the end of the experiment, those who imagined they were physically younger showed signs of de-aging. Blood pressure was lowered, arthritis was diminished, and even eyesight and hearing in this control group improved.

By simply imagining themselves younger, some physical aging was actually reversed. Their thoughts made this happen.

3. The Water Experiments

The most famous experiment that proves the power of thought was carried out by Dr. Masaru Emoto. He photographed frozen water crystals after thoughts of love and peace or hate and fear were projected onto them. Sometimes the intentions were spoken out loud, while other times the intentions were merely thought.

The results were always the same. Messages of hope, peace, love, joy and the like resulted in beautiful, symmetrical crystals, while messages of fear, hate, anger, sadness and the like resulted in disjointed and broken crystals. His experiments proved that our intentions can physically alter the world around us.

4. Resonance Theory Of Consciousness

Einstein once stated that everything is energy, and modern scientists elaborate that it's all about vibrations.

While the LoA basically explains that human consciousness is in constant synchronization with the Universal higher consciousness, in fact, a resonance is at the heart not only of human consciousness but of physical reality in general.

Tam Hunt and Jonathan Schooler, of the University of California, Santa Barbara, developed the "resonance theory of consciousness" that suggests that all things in our universe are constantly vibrating and attracting things of the same frequency. This is described today as the phenomenon of spontaneous self-organization. In other words, your consciousness is constantly syncing up with the world around you and organizing things in your life in resonance with your vibrations.

5. How Order Emerges from Chaos in the Universe, Nature, and Daily Life

Steven Strogatz, a leading mathematician in the fields of chaos and complexity theory, in his book Sync explains how synchrony works across multiple systems on micro and macro levels. He provides various examples of resonance from physics, biology, chemistry and neuroscience to illustrate synchrony, including:

- Fireflies of certain species flash their little fires in synchronization with large gatherings of fireflies.

- Human brains can kickstart large-scale neuron firing at specific frequencies called a neuronal synchrony
- When photons of the same power and frequency are in synchronization, they produce lasers.
- The moon's rotation is exactly synced with its orbit around the Earth such that we always see the same face.

How To Use The Law Of Attraction (And What For)?

The Law of Attraction is a universal principle that is already working in your life. Start intentionally thinking about what you want to attract into your life, such as money, love, and relationships, health, and spirituality, to make the Law of Attraction work for you.

Before we get down to the details, it's important to clarify some crucial moments that can't be bypassed when it comes to the Law of Attraction.

The Law of Attraction is just one of the laws that govern our universe. There are others, like the law of gravity, for example. You can't defy the other laws of the universe, so don't expect to. In that way, no, you can't make just anything happen.

What Principles Shall I Observe When It Comes To The Law Of Attraction?

Free Will

Everything in this Universe has free will. In other words, your desires and manifestations must follow this principle. You can master the Law of Attraction and attract whatever you wish for, but if it violates somebody's free will, it will not serve you well.

Your Intentions Vs Other People's Intentions

You're also competing with other people's intentions – both good and bad. So, be aware that if your desire is in direct conflict with someone else's stronger desire, the universe will respond accordingly. The Law of Attraction does not give you full and total control of your life, it simply states that like will attract like. And you can use this to your advantage by being intentional with your desires, but this isn't magic.

Law Of Resonance

There is another law that comes hand in hand with the LoA – that's the Law of Resonance. Alike attracts alike and on top of that things tend to vibrate on the same frequency so the prevailing vibration will win over the rest.

For example, if you work on manifesting abundance but on a subconscious level you are wired around scarcity and fears, then you will keep attracting scarcity and lack that serve as a magnet.

Now that you understand what the Law of Attraction is and how it works, let's talk about the ways you can use it to improve your life.

1. Attract Money

Financial abundance is the number one reason people become interested in the Law of Attraction. It's no wonder. Working tirelessly for small paychecks is exhausting and when life starts throwing unexpected expenses your way, debt can seem inevitable.

The good news is that the Law of Attraction money is easy to come by. Once you learn the techniques, you'll start to see changes really quickly. Many people report unexpected checks, seemingly random job opportunities and even literally finding money as some of the first results when working with the Law of Attraction.

2. Manifest Love And Relationships

The second most popular reason people seek information about the Law of Attraction is to find true love. Finding a lifetime partner to fulfill an ideal, loving relationship can seem like an elusive and frustrating game that you can't win.

Luckily, the Law of Attraction is a great tool for finding love. Because the Law of Attraction means working on yourself and your desires, it inherently makes you a more attractive person with a clear vision of what you want and need in your life.

3. Improve Your Health

Most people don't consider using the Law of Attraction to bring better health into their lives, but as you noticed in the results of the aging experiment, it's actually a great tool for that purpose. Because the Law of Attraction works with thoughts and thoughts affect our physical reality, you may be attracting poor health into your life right now without even realizing it.

Learning about the Law of Attraction helps you see that your thoughts are having a direct effect on your entire world — including the vessel you're traveling in. A good attitude goes a long way to improving your health, and the Law of Attraction can help you take that even further.

4. Spiritual Awakening

By its very nature, the Law of Attraction connects you with higher, spiritual planes of existence. When you start practicing the techniques, you begin to see beyond the mundane, ordinary world. A new, brighter world opens up to you that is brimming with possibility.

Many people find a spiritual awakening in those possibilities. Connecting with the rhythms of the universe and opening up to new potentials awakens the spiritual force inside you that is connected to everything around you. The Law of Attraction demonstrates that you are connected to everything and everything is connected to you.

5. Have More Fun

The results of using the Law of Attraction techniques are only limited by your imagination (and by the laws of physics, you're not going to manifest bird-like flying anytime soon).

There are endless things you can attract in your life. From practical things — like "good parking karma" that can guarantee you a great parking spot, to "calls to adventure" that open you up to random invitations to explore the world — you can use the principles behind the Law of Attraction in any way you please.

4 Steps To Work With The Law Of Attraction

By now, you understand what the Law of Attraction is and how it can work in your life, so now it's time to start practicing the techniques. In this section, you're going to learn the 4-step process to transform your dreams from a mere desire to actual reality.

As we walk through each step, we'll explain its importance and how to ensure you're doing it right. Together we'll dive deeply into the process to understand the merits of each step.

Before you begin:

The possibilities for attraction with the Law of Attraction are only limited by your imagination. Start thoughtfully. It's important to take time to think about the process where your life is now and where you want it to be.

The foundation of the Law of Attraction is to believe that it actually works. Try out the techniques on small things first. To get a feel for how the law can work in your life, choose something minor that seems possible. If you have your doubts, test it out with something simple – this is your first step to master the Law of Attraction!

Small things can include parking spots, randomly finding $10, or hearing from an old friend. These are great to start out with because it is easyier to believe in them. Once the result happens, it will reaffirm your belief in the Law of Attraction and you can move on to something bigger.

Let's walk through the 4-step process to transform your dreams from a mere desire to actual reality.

Step 1: Make Your Decision

Deciding what you want is the first and most critical step in the Law of Attraction. You need a really clear vision of your desire. Whether you wish to attract something minor, or you're looking for a huge overhaul of your life, be clear about what you truly want.

When you imagine this new "thing" in your life, imagine it fully with each of your five senses. Spend time in quiet meditation imaging your life after you've attracted this new thing. Whether it's as simple as finding $10 or as profound as bumping into your one, true love on the street, feel this new thing with every part of your being.

Imagine what this new thing looks like, smells like, sounds like, feels like and tastes like if it's relevant.

- How do you feel once this new thing is in your life?
- Where do you feel it in your body?
- Does it make your toes tingle or make your heart flutter?
- Does your pulse race or do you feel a wave of calm?

Make it real in your mind. Don't just focus your thoughts on receiving this new thing, think about your life after it too. Imagine how it will change your world.

Step 1 is important because it prepares your mind and body to receive whatever you're asking for. Our brains don't know the difference between reality and imagination.

When you engage in full, sensory imagination, your brain fires up your body to move forward. Muscles, blood flow, heart, lungs and every part of your body gear up to take part in whatever you're imagining.

Taking part in this imagination exercise, you align yourself with your desires. Open up to the possibilities and prepare your body to receive whatever it is you are attempting to attract. It may seem simple, but this first step is what paves the way to working with the energies of the Law of Attraction.

Step 2: Practice Unconditional Love

Simply put, if you don't believe you deserve what you're seeking, you're not going to get it. Those deep, subconscious fears and doubts send messages loud and clear too. If part of you feels as though you don't deserve what you're seeking, then that part of you is competing with your desire.

Think of it as a radio signal. As you scan through the radio, in-between stations fight for a signal. Most people are pretty familiar with this experience. The two stations compete and occasionally you'll hear one song and then parts of a different song start to edge in. You'll notice that neither station comes in perfectly crisp and clear. In the same manner, when you experience doubt or fear, those thoughts and feelings interrupt and compete with your desires.

It's difficult to free yourself completely from doubt, fear or feeling as though you don't deserve something. And your instinct might try to combat those feelings using negative thoughts like, "Don't be afraid" or even direct conflicts like, "You deserve this."

But such methods are ineffective and simply don't work because they reinforce negative thoughts and feelings.

Step 2 is important because it brings awareness of our thoughts and feelings. The only effective method for combating fears and doubts is to become aware of them, acknowledge them and approach them with love and compassion.

You experience those feelings for a deep-seated reason. Something someone told you, or the result of something you did, made you feel unworthy. That's painful, so, of course, you feel afraid or doubtful.

This step is important because those competing signals can be quite strong, but you can weaken the signal or change the direction of those thoughts like this -- approach those feelings with the love and compassion that you would feel toward a lonely, small child or a hurt animal. When you love yourself, you open up the possibility to receive your greatest desires, and you begin to only desire the things that are best for you.

Step 3: Open Up To The Possibilities

Addressing your fears and doubts is important. But after a brief acknowledgment, replace those fears and doubts with appreciation and gratitude. These new, positive feelings change your perspective and expectations, opening up to the possibility that more great things are on your horizon.

Perhaps you don't see how the Law of Attraction has worked for you in the past. You can hope and dream and intend all day long, but at some point, you've got to step back.

So, let's conduct a comparison.

First, think about the bad things in your life right now. Can you see connections to your fears, doubts, and old patterns that led those things into your life?

Focus on understanding your part in this overall process, rather than feeling guilty or ashamed. Recognizing how your fears have manifested in your life does not mean that the bad things in your life are your fault. It simply means that the Law of Attraction has responded to the signal you sent out. Just acknowledge that the system works and your new awareness will guide you. No need to shame yourself or even feel responsible.

Next, think of all the great things in your life. Reflect upon how your hopes, dreams, and ambition attracted those good things to you. Reinforce in your mind how, when you believe something can happen, it does.

Again, rather than experiencing pride or feeling boastful, this is about understanding and seeing how the Law of Attraction is already a part of your life. It's always existed, but now you are aware of it.

Step 3 is important because of connections, awareness, and gratitude. Cataloging every little thing in your life and tracing it back to a thought or feeling is time-consuming and not helpful. Instead, make connections to where you are now and the state of your mind that led you there.

Once you see that the Law of Attraction works without you knowing, it will reinforce your understanding that this is simply a universal law. Work with your awareness of the law and understand how it works. Then you can work with the law and align yourself with it.

Finally, invest the effort to express gratitude.

Feel grateful and appreciative for how this law has already worked so well for you. Make a list of all the great things in your life and express your appreciation for those things. Expressing gratitude is the key to setting yourself up for more and better things.

Step 4: Experience The Reality Of Your Desires

Now, it's time to live the reality of your desires. You've imagined what you want, cleared away your doubts and fears and realized how the law has already worked for you in the past. You practiced this type of imagination exercise in Step 1, but now it's time to live out that imagination.

This is a bit of an acting exercise, so let go of your inhibitions to make this exercise really effective. Rather than just visualizing the reality in your mind, live it as much as possible. This may feel silly or strange to you, but in a moment, we will explain why it's so important.

If you're practicing these techniques with something simple, it's time to take action and expect your results.

If you're using the system to find great parking, get in your car and drive to that parking spot with the full intention and expectation of finding it clear for you. Announce it out loud. "That parking spot is clear for me. I am parking in a spot that is open for me." Again, we are fully aware that this seems really silly, but it's a critical step.

If you're practicing the technique on something bigger, this exercise may be tricky, but use your imagination. For example, if you're trying to lose weight, go out and buy an outfit that fits the size you're aiming for. If you want a new car, go to a dealership and shop around. Or, if you're aiming for something as big as complete financial freedom, start planning what you're going to do with all that free time and money.

The important step is to take action and act as if you already have what you're looking for. It doesn't need to be extravagant.

Step 4 is important for two reasons. The first is that it aligns you with your desires. The entire concept behind the Law of Attraction is that like attracts like. When you take action as if you've already gotten what you desire, you are sending a huge, loud, and clear message to the universe that you're serious. Actions speak louder than words, right?

Also, this step is important because it allows you to really feel the gratification of what it's like when you've attracted your desire. It solidifies your belief and reinforces the visualization you worked on in the first step. Jump into this final step with joy and enthusiasm.

Why Persistence Is The Key To The Law Of Attraction

So, after you've completed the four steps, you'll probably ask, "Now what?"

The final piece to the Law of Attraction puzzle is persistence.

There's no formula for how long things take to manifest into your life. We each have our own individual hurdles to overcome, and it will take time to see the results of this system.

Some people begin to see things happen immediately, while others take a little more time. But the key here is patience and persistence.

As soon as doubt or fear start to creep back in, return to Step 2 and address it. If you have lost touch with your clear intention, revert to Step 1. If your belief in the Law of Attraction lags, go back to Step 3. And if all else fails, repeat Step 4 every day until it becomes a reality!

Continue to express gratitude and appreciation every day. Think positively and recall all the connections you made that prove the Law of Attraction is real for you. Take time every day to review the visualization exercises and prep your mind and body to receive this incredible gift.

The Law of Attraction is universal and it's going to work with or without your intention. If you keep coming up short, address those doubts and fears because they're likely speaking to you much louder than your desires.

We've said it before, but it's worth repeating. The Law of Attraction is a universal law that's going to work with or without your permission. Your awareness of it and understanding of how it can work in your life will attract more of the things that you desire.

But, it's hard to get used to using the right mindset and sending out the right signals. Whether you're unsure how to get a really clear vision of what you want or you're struggling to release the fears and doubts that seem to speak louder than you, we've come up with a list of exercises to help you.

Exercises That Help You Attract What You Desire

Practice any and all of the exercises you want to. Try every exercise at least once. There are no hard and fast rules, so feel free to tweak these exercises and make them your own. These are aids to help you overcome any challenges you might face while attempting to work with the Law of Attraction.

1. Vision Boards

Vision boards have become a really popular exercise for figuring out exactly what you want in your life. In their simplest form, these boards contain images and words that resonate with what you want to attract your way.

There are two great results from making vision boards. First, the act of spending time finding images and words and attaching them to a board is a personal commitment to your desires. It helps you clarify what you really want, visualize it and put energy toward making it real.

Second, the images serve as a great reminder of your desires. Each day, you can look at the board and remind yourself of what you're trying to attract.

Creating a vision board is easy. Go through magazines or search the internet to find images that represent what you want to attract. And it doesn't matter if the images are metaphorical or literal. The important thing is that the images speak to you and connect with your desires. Attach the images to a board and place it in a prominent place where you will look at it every day.

2. Sensory Visualization

Some people are blessed with a vivid imagination, which makes Step 1 really easy. For others, who have a difficult time actually sensing and feeling their desires, this exercise is for you.

If you have trouble visualizing your desires, start small and work your way up. Close your eyes and visualize a piece of fruit. For some reason, an orange works best, but if you hate oranges, definitely choose something else. For the purposes of this example, we'll imagine an orange. Follow this simple exercise:

- Close your eyes and see the fruit in your mind's eye. Picture it as clearly as you can. See the imperfect, round shape; the bright, orange color; and the dimpled, waxy texture.
- Imagine holding the orange. How does it feel in your hands? See yourself examining it, rubbing it, bouncing it up and down in your hand. Feel its weight. Is it cold or room temperature?
- Smell the orange. Use your memory to engage your sense of smell and see if you can smell the orange. Can you smell that familiar scent? Breathe in deeply and take in the smell.
- Gently tap the orange on a surface near you. What sound does it make? Flick it with your thumb and pointer finger. Can you hear it? Keep trying until you hear it clearly.
- Peel the orange. Hear the sound of the peel ripping from the flesh. See the white rind on the back of the peel. See the shiny, wet pulp beginning to emerge. Smell the sweet, citrus smell getting much stronger.
- Take a bite. Feel the texture of the orange in your mouth. Feel the juice and the cold flesh on your tongue. Taste the sweet and satisfying flavor.

Try this exercise with anything, and once you've mastered it, Step 1 of the Law of Attraction techniques becomes much easier. Improve visualization by recording your voice reading the exercise out loud and then playing it back with your eyes closed and concentrating on the techniques.

3. Gratitude List

We talked about the importance of gratitude in Step 3, but we're going to dive a little deeper here. Gratitude sets you up for success because it places you in the right mindset to receive it.

Expect that the universe is more likely to give you things if you're already grateful for what it has provided to you. Giving an asked-for birthday gift to someone and barely receiving a thank you, you'd likely avoid providing a second gift. But on the other hand, you'd get excited about giving a repeat gift to someone who enthusiastically expressed their appreciation for your gift. Imagine the universe in the same way.

Make a gratitude list to help with sourcing and expressing gratitude. Here are a couple ways to do this:

- Make a huge list of all the things you're thankful for. Add to the list whenever you think of something else.
- Make a list every night (or every morning) of some things you appreciate in your life right now.

Imagine waking up every morning and reading a list of the great things in your life right now. It would definitely put you in a better mood and shift your perspective to find other things that make you happy. Like attracts like.

4. Mindfulness

Mindfulness is the practice of self-awareness without judgment. When you are mindful, you aren't just aware of what you're feeling and thinking, you're observing it without analyzing it.

- Mindfulness isn't, "My hands are shaky because I'm afraid of this meeting. I shouldn't be afraid. There's nothing to fear."
- Rather, mindfulness is, "I feel afraid of how others will think about me in this meeting. I feel afraid of embarrassing myself. My hands are shaking as a result of this fear."

It's crucial to understand that mindfulness isn't about changing anything or trying to understand it. This is because the analytical and judgment aspects, our automatic reactions, are unhealthy and actually perpetuate the problem. It reinforces the connection in our brain between the action and the negative feeling. To release that connection, approach it without judgment. Let it be.

There's a lot of scientific research behind the effects of mindfulness, and it's well beyond the scope of this guide. What you should know is that mindfulness is proven to relieve things like anxiety and depression and has an incredibly beneficial effect on things like blood pressure, the immune system, heart rate, and even cancer.

Mindfulness is an important part of the Law of Attraction because it takes self-awareness in the absence of judgment to get what you want.

For true awareness of what you want, also know your fears and the signals those fears are sending out to the universe. To change them, approach these fears and signals with love and compassion. The next exercise is for this purpose.

5. Loving Kindness Meditation

Approaching your fears and doubts with love and compassion is difficult. Negative emotions are quite overpowering and limiting, and as a result, are hard to feel a lot of love for. Have patience with yourself and try out a loving kindness meditation.

Loving Kindness Meditation is a Buddhist meditation that sends out compassion to yourself, others, and the entire world. And it is a great way to put your mind in a place that easily gives and receives loves.

Simply find the feeling of compassion within yourself and let it radiate to others. To perform this meditation, imagine the warmth and desire that stirs within you to help a small child or an injured animal and allow that to radiate from you.

6. Be Intentional

The majority of us walk around performing daily actions without intention. We get up, get ready for our day, and go about our day not really thinking about our actions. And too often, our distracted thoughts and feelings drift away from the action we're performing.

To really work with the Law of Attraction, be intentional with your thoughts, feelings, and actions. Intention focuses your brain activity and uses every available resource to help you perform an action. This type of disciplined focus will help you achieve faster and more accurate results when using the Law of Attraction.

So, to practice being intentional, simply focus on an everyday activity and set your intention on each action you perform on that task. At first, the practice will feel overwhelmingly tedious, but just keep practicing and watch how your focus shifts to the reality of the moment.

For example, do the dishes tonight with intention. Before you take any action, speak your intention out loud (or in your mind, if you've got company). Say,

- "I am going to make this dish clean again."
- "I pick up the dish."
- "I'm turning on the hot water."
- "I am putting soap on the sponge."

Don't take any action without first announcing your intention to take that action. Again, it feels tedious at first, but soon, you'll notice something incredible -- the simple act of washing a dish is really a series of several actions, movements, and thoughts. And when your intention is focused on the action, you'll appreciate exactly how much movement is involved.

Normally, a person approaches such an action on autopilot, but stepping back, you'll notice the entirety of the series of decisions and actions that make up your very, full day when you move with intention.

7. Try Affirmations

Affirmations work wonderfully for many people who start out with the Law of Attraction. And there are plenty of Law of Attraction affirmations that you can try out for yourself!

8. Free Your Body

Fling your inhibitions into the wind! Practice freeing your body and dance like nobody's watching.

This final exercise can help you overcome inhibitions that make this final step feel really silly. Some people struggle with feelings of embarrassment and shame, even when alone. But what's the harm in acting out an imaginary scenario when no one is there to witness it? It still feels silly, doesn't it?

We get used to thinking and caring about what people think about us. And even when we're alone, we're so conditioned to worry about our image that we often inhibit even our solitary actions.

So, practice freeing your body. Dance like nobody's watching. That's all it takes to make this exercise work. Find a place where you can be alone and just let loose. Music or no music, let your body move however it wants to. Don't think. Just do.

CHAPTER THREE

THE ART OF SELF-HELP

There are still not that many self-help programmes for self-esteem on the market, but fortunately, awareness about self-esteem is increasing and the number of self-esteem self-help programmes are increasing too. In order to help you to decide which programme to choose I will write about some different aspects that can be good to keep in mind when you are looking for a self-esteem self-help programme.

First of all, you need to be aware of what it is that you want to get out of the self-esteem home study course or self-esteem distance course. Do you want to know why your self-esteem has become as it is today? Do you want learn practical self-esteem exercises? Do you prefer writing exercises? Do you want to learn about the different aspects of your self-esteem and about which aspect that is most beneficial for you to focus on? Once you know exactly what it is that you want to get out of the self-help programme you can start to evaluate whether the specific programme that you are looking at will fulfill your wishes. Compare the programmes to make sure that you get the mixture that you want.

You also need to decide in which way you would like to learn? For example, if you like learning from videos, my 10-week distance course in self-esteem would be good. If you like doing pen and paper exercises, then one of the Self-esteem Toolkits would be better. Also, do you want your programme to include personal one-to-one support or do you want to do it all anonymously on your own?

Making efforts to improve one-self is a very personal and conscious choice. The human potential is infinite. Growing and developing is an individual goal. As far as my knowledge goes, all successful persons from Albert Einstein to Bill Gates have continuously focused and strived hard to achieve their ambitions. To become a better person it is imperative to grow and develop constantly. Browsing through self-improvement sites and arriving at this page is in itself taking the first step towards trying to improve your-self. Congratulations! And read further to become a better individual.

The journey of self-improvement does not stop with just one or a few achievements. Pursuing active growth processes is the quality of a true winner. Great people, whether scientists or musicians or creative people keep saying, "I am still learning." This phrase is quite common in people in their sixties/seventies/eighties. Younger adults are more head-strong and are hesitant to be humble.

Being an academic professional for more than a decade and a writer, my experience suggests the following three self-help measures to improve self-esteem.

1. SELF-ESTEEM: Self-esteem can be defined as the 'feeling about self.' It is generally influenced by ones perceptions, thought process and experiences. Self-esteem is nurtured right from childhood and shaped through different phases of life. Good experiences backed by close and strong relations with kith and kin positively build our esteem. While criticism or teasing can have a negative impact.

Higher self-esteem is the driving force to achieving success in life. However, everyone is not fortunate to have an inborn quality of high self-esteem. It needs to be built with conscious effort. The first step towards developing a positive self-esteem is to feel great about oneself and begin with the task of setting a goal for oneself.

The feeling of 'it is not my cup of tea' or 'maybe I cannot do it' is a setback. Delete such phrases from the mind. Great achievers have stumbled and fallen before claiming a name for themselves. Apart from a positive attitude, extension of self-imposed limitations and commitment are steps in furthering the esteem process. Inspite of hurdles march ahead aiming at the goal and pat your-self with each forward step. This definitely will boost your spirit. (BELIEVE IN YOURSELF)

2. SELF-MOTIVATION: Once the first step of believing in oneself is taken, the second step of self-improvement is self-motivation. Motivation is a force that drives one to achieve success. It is an action taken in leaps and bounds to diminish distance from goal. Motivation is both internal and external. Internal motivation is an innate force that is intangible and permanent. External motivation relies largely on perks and incentives and is short-term. Complacency is the greatest hurdle to self motivation. A self-satisfied person does not grow further and in fact reaches a dead end.

Motivation needs to be fuelled constantly to achieve success. Taking up responsibility and being recognized for that are great motivating factors. Avoid ambiguity and confusion, instead focus on the goal. Devise ways to achieve the ultimate goal. Remember action in a particular direction is effective than aimless action. Develop achievable, time bound strategies that lead to fulfilling aspirations and aims.

3. SELF-CONFIDENCE: The final step in self-improvement is boosting ones self-confidence. The true qualities of a self-confident person can be summed up as; setting goals, committing to achieve them, taking responsibilities, and bearing the consequences as well as the fruits of success.

Learning and growing doesn't stop with age or the number of achievements. It is the zeal to do more and achieve more keeps a self confident person alive. Set aside failures and pitfalls and move ahead with a strong conviction. Tread on hurdles with a positive outlook.

New Way Of Life With Self-Help

The culture of the 21st century is toward individuals being more self-aware, self-efficient and self-empowered.

One of the vehicles we are using toward this is self-help. There has been reports of an increase in self-help books and other materials that flood book stores and websites. There seems to be no end to the modern person's need toward self-actualization. Though self actualization is often a process and not necessarily a destination, self-efficiency would certainly be one of the modern person's most prized life skills. Self-help can range from medication to service options. Self-help has become the culture of our time.

We can be part of self help group that can help us deal with issues such as depression or even alcohol abuse. Self-awareness usually goes before self-help when the individual realizes a need to grow, develop or as Maslow's Hierarchy indicates, self-actualize. Some would argue that the success or even option of self-help depends entirely on the individual as there are some people who are more independent than others in taking initiative in seeking help. The options that these independent individuals usually opt for is self help. Can self-help be a dependable option for all things, or would one at some point need the direct assistance and help of those in the know? Personally, I think that self-help works best when facilitated by an expert in a particular field of interest. Let's use our self-help group who deal with depression for example. At some point the input of a professional mental health expert would be needed. The expert may devise proven coping mechanisms for the participants to apply in their daily life to be able to better cope with bouts of depression as they occur.

Throughout the self-help programme, the professional mental health expert could also play an important role in monitoring progress or the further development of the participant. In my opinion, self-help is a great option, and this option is coupled with the facilitative role of an expert, the benefits can be rewarding to the individual. Without this kind of facilitation, the possibility or risk of the individual derailing from very useful guidelines is present. Facilitation of expertise help can assist the participant in further development as well as raise their self-empowerment. A self empowered individual may in turn possess the self confidence needed to fully utilize or even create opportunities. However, the need for self-empowerment, can vary from one person to the next.

We are all, to a great degree, ever changing individuals living in an ever changing world. If we were to use a self-help approach toward self-actualization, it could very well become one of the best tools our generation may develop for the future of our children. Nurturing the reliance on one's own efforts and abilities in order to solve problems instead of complete dependence upon others could be of tremendous value to human development.

Don't Worry Be Happy - If you Aren't Happy Then What Are You?

Live life to the fullest, spread your arms and breathe, don't be afraid of change, the world is for you to have not the other way around. Use the power of your mind to free yourself from the shackles of negativity.

Life is to short to be unhappy stop wasting time on negative impulse. Take negativity and use it as fuel for positive thought.

Where To Make The Change

Self help deals mostly with the concept of self-development. Development of the self occurs in various stages and incorporates many facets that need to be explored. Self-help can be understood as the furthering of development of the self through self-realisation, self-actualisation and exploring of the self. We as humans have the ability to change aspects of ourselves that we may be unhappy with. The ability to change these aspects of ourselves and incorporate characteristics will ultimately empower us and the way we think of ourselves. Self-help is more of a psychological endeavour than anything else and thus may take time to identify what we need help with and how to begin the process of the developing ourselves. Many times, self-help can be gotten from books that specialise on the topic or from certified therapists who are able to guide you through the process.

If you have decided to embark on the journey of self-development, it is important to remember some key fundamental aspects that you will need to consider from the very beginning. For one, you need to become your own self-evaluator of sorts, so exactly what is it you wish to develop or change about yourself? Secondly, are you able to maintain an objective stance towards your own development? Are you able to survey your changes that are going to be conducive to your ultimate growth?

The ability to honestly evaluate who you are and the changes you wish to make is already a huge step in the self-development process. The ability to challenge yourself is the aim of self-help and in this way, change the aspects of yourself which will make you feel better as a person. In order to begin the self-help process, you need to critically analyze facets of your life that you feel may need changing.

Look at the following list of aspects and ask yourself if this is where the change needs to be made:

- Morals and Values
- Stress, anxiety and fears
- Dependency on persons or substances
- Anger and rage
- Understanding of ourselves and loved ones
- Depression, happiness or ideas of the self

- Expectations
- Self-control

This is just to list a few of the concepts that you will need to look at in order to ascertain exactly where you think you need help. Once you have noted the things you would like to work on, you need to create a list of priorities and begin to slowly work toward facing and dealing with the challenges at hand. Remember, this process may result in you feeling more vulnerable or insecure than when you first started but admitting the changes that need to me made is the first step to self-realisation.

Self-realisation is an act of introspection that occurs when we gain insight into ourselves by being willing to work hard at self-development. It occurs when we are strong enough to thoroughly unpack the good as well as the bad aspects of ourself. Once you have laid it out in front of you to examine, you can properly begin to work out and sift through what is both quite unnecessarily and undeniably important. Remember that this process can be both painful and most enlightening and exhilarating at the same time!

Once you have begun the self-help process, you will realise that you are a beautiful individual just waiting to be realized by not only others, but yourself and this realisation process begins with you having a strong and hard look in the mirror. Self-help equals self-love.

Self-discipline Coaching:

Do you remember Stuart Smalley from Saturday Night Live? He was a character that took the idea of self-help and made fun of it. Stuart would look in the mirror and tell himself he was special and smart and do other daily affirmations. A famous quote that he said is, "... because I'm good enough, I'm smart enough, and doggonit, people like me!"

The most interesting thing about this skit is that even though they sought to make fun of the entire self-help movement, there was truth in what they did. The more you talk to yourself in a positive way, the more positive your life will become and the more successful you will become. It's just a fact that positive people are often more successful than negative people. The reason is that positive people believe they deserve to be successful.

- **No One Knows You Better Than Yourself** - Also, no one is more judgmental to you than yourself. It's sad that the one person you can truly count on, turns on you and treats you worse than you would allow any other individual to treat you, isn't it? But you can turn this around by taking hold of the idea of self-help and realizing that it's not just a comedy skit. It's real, and it can affect your entire being -- mind, body and spirit.
- **Believe in Self-Help** - People who are interested in self-help are generally open-minded people who believe that they have some measure of control over what happens to them. That means that people who get help from self-help already believe that it is possible. They are willing to give the suggestions they learn a try, and due to that fact alone usually see success in their efforts.
- **Self-Help Can Build Self-Confidence** - When you feel confident in yourself, positive things begin to happen to your mind. If you previously thought you could not do something and found that you could after reading a self-help book, it means that you went outside of your comfort zone and experienced success. It is likely that the self-confidence you developed will wash over into trying more new things. It can be like a snowball effect that more confidence builds more confidence.
- **Self-Help Can Reduce Anxiety** - When you realize that you're not helpless against your emotions and feelings, you will start to notice a big change. When you manage to overcome some of your social anxiety due to taking some of the actions you've read about in self-help books, then each step you take out of anxiety will get easier. This isn't to say that you will never need medication for social

anxiety, but you might realize from self-help that it's okay to take medication if you need it.
- **Self-Help Can Be the Catalyst for Getting Healthy** - Very few people are able to change their body through diet and exercise, because they don't think that they can or they haven't figured out a plan of action to do it. By reading self-help books and finding stories of others who have accomplished it, you start to realize it is possible and that you can do it too. Even if you only reach half your goal, you will still end up healthier than before self-help.
- **Self-Help Makes It Normal to Be Spiritual** - Today it can be hard to be spiritual due to how busy everyone is and how it feels like a dog-eat-dog world which is full of anything but love. But when you read self-help books and try to practice self-love and acceptance, you start realizing how much you need the spiritual food that love gives you. When you make it a priority, your life will become better.

While many people treat self-help like a joke, it is actually very effective in helping a lot of people make their lives better. People do not come away from a study of self-help in any area of life unchanged. Taking the time to learn is always going to be a good thing.

CHAPTER FOUR

SELF-CARE TIPS

Whilst self care might seem like a millennial buzzword, the concept of prioritizing and taking time for yourself has been around for centuries. Philosophers like Plato proclaimed the benefits of reflection and contemplation. Mindfulness has its roots in Buddhism. Ancient Greeks were all about self-love – or Philautia, as they called it then. So, whilst it seems to be a hot topic in 2019, it is certainly not a new idea.

But what is self care? The dictionary defines it as 'the practice of taking an active role in protecting one's own well-being and happiness,' which summarises the modern take on it. It also mentions that this is particularly important at periods of high stress. As it feels like the entire planet (including the climate) are feeling strained at the moment, it's maybe unsurprising that Google searches for self-care have doubled over the last two years.

What a person defines as their version of self-care changes from individual to individual. For some it's a bubble bath and a good book, for others it's a kale smoothie and 1000 burpees. However, you choose to do it, at its core self-care is all about listening to what your mind and body needs and giving it to yourself, guilt free.

Why is self-care so important?

In a busy modern world, it's important to remember to look after our base needs as humans. We need healthy food, we need to feel safe and we need to rest. It's very easy to lose sight of these primal requirements when we're surrounded by technology, and leading hectic lives.

However, the instant gratification of scrolling through social media might give you a hit of dopamine, but it isn't enriching your sense of self. Self-care is often about disconnecting with the world – both physically and virtually – and putting your needs first.

But sometimes we can feel guilty when we do things for ourselves. It's easy to think that you "should" be working, doing those household chores, calling a family member, etc. But in fact taking the time to look after our emotional health means you will be productive when you're working, better able to care for others and most importantly, you'll feel better. It's an important investment, and one that we often neglect with our hectic 24/7 lifestyles.

Self-care is especially important for those with stressful jobs, like social workers, nurses and teachers. It's also a crucial part of a preconception care. If you are a parent or mum, or hoping to become one, creating a robust self care routine is strongly advised. Fertility and stress are intrinsically linked, so it could also help increase your chances of conceiving.

Having a good self-care routine will also help nurture your good relationships with others. Imagine a "care cup," it's important to keep our care cup topped up. You may have heard the phrase "you can't pour from empty." While it may sound cliche, there's a lot of truth in this phrase. If we are not taking the time to look after ourselves and are stressed, tired, overwhelmed, you are much less likely to have the resilience to cope when times are tougher.

Self-care package

Self-care is all part of a healthy lifestyle. Here are some key elements of self-care and tips on how you can incorporate them in to your daily life.

Sleep

Most people need around 7-8 hour of quality sleep to function healthily, so this should be a priority. The body not only needs sleep to regenerate and create energy but it's also processing everything that has happened that day. This is important from a self-care and mental health perspective. Our capacity to manage our emotions dramatically diminishes when we're not getting enough sleep. Sleep is truly a cornerstone human health, there are even studies that show there are more heart attacks on the days when the clocks skip forward!

Self-care Tips: Go to bed an hour earlier than usual and read book rather than scrolling through your phone. For extra special self care, sprinkle some lavender oil on your pillow!

Have a healthy, nutritious diet

As with all elements of self-care, your diet is about balance. Aiming to eat healthily is not about trying to lose weight or trying to look a certain way. It's about listening to your body and understanding what it needs to be nurtured.

Fat diets, junk food, and binge drinking are all part of the culture of instant gratification, that is not sustainable. A sugar high will inevitably lead to a crash and a fad diet will almost always lead to you feeling worse, rather than better about your body. If you listen to what your body wants, most of the time it will be craving nutritious, vitamin rich foods – as well as the occasional cookie!

Self-care Tips: Treat yourself to a night in trying out new, healthy recipes. Make it an enjoyable activity that you're excited about rather than a laborious task. If you need some inspiration, check out our fertility diet plan. The recipes are great even if you're not trying for a baby!

Exercise regularly

The physical benefits of exercise have long been recognised. However, in recent years the positive impact it has on your mental health has become more widely understood. Even if the idea of the gym makes you want to hide under the covers, you won't regret getting active.

30 minutes of physical activity a day is enough to get endorphins running around your body and give you a sense of achievement – both great for self-care.

Self-care Tips: Don't force yourself to do something you hate, find an activity that puts a smile on your face. Dance around your kitchen to your favourite song, take a brisk walk in the woods or do some skipping!

Go to yoga

At Adia, we are huge fans of yoga and talk a lot about yoga for fertility. But yoga is also a great part of a self-care routine, whether or not you are trying to conceive. The practice of yoga really connects the body, mind, and soul. The physical side of it will form part of your essential daily activity, but it will also give you so much more. Yoga is great for mental health and can help with stress and anxiety, give you time to reflect and get in touch with yourself.

Self-care Tips: If you don't feel comfortable joining a class, there are great Youtube vides you can follow. Why not create your own little yoga studio at home with a mat, candles, and incense?

Practice meditation

Many people put yoga and meditation in the same bracket and whilst they definitely can be practiced together, they aren't exactly the same. You can actually meditate anywhere, even on a busy packed train, and its a great part of self-care. The whole point of mindfulness meditation is to be present, and to allow yourself to focus on your breathing and your body.

Whilst ideally it's wonderful to take some time out, and have peace and quiet, to meditate, there are other ways. You can bring mediation in to your everyday life by practicing mindfulness. You won't realise it but you will often undertake daily tasks whilst thinking about something completely different. With mindfulness, you stay completely focused on the task in hand.

Self-care Tips: Meditate whilst you're making a cup of tea! Focus on the sound of the kettle boiling, how the water changes colour and the smell coming from your mug.

Spend time with your family and friends

As discussed earlier, part of self-care is learning when to say no to people and to take some time for yourself. However, it's also important to spend time with loved ones, as isolation can impact your mental wellbeing. But be mindful of who you surround yourself with.

You want to ensure your friends are bringing a positive energy and are adding value and love to your life. It's very easy to fall into negative patterns and to continue giving your time to toxic people who don't give back. Regularly check in with yourself and think about how you spend your time and who with. Be grateful and nurture relationships with the people who make you happy and let the negative people go.

Self-care Tips: Write a list of the ten people that make you the happiest and who enrich your life. Include people you see all the time and maybe some you have lost contact with. Then arrange times to catch up with each of them regularly throughout the year.

Take time away from work

Whilst technology has undoubtedly made our lives, both professional and personal, easier, it comes with its drawbacks. In a modern world where we are constantly connected, it can be hard to shut off, even after leaving the office.

For the increasing amount of people joining the gig economy and working for themselves, this balance is even harder to strike. Set clear boundaries with your managers and clients, so they don't expect you to respond to emails on weekends. Working and looking at your screen late in the evening will disrupt your sleep. It's important to set aside a few hours in the evening that are dedicated to screen-free activities.

Self-care Tip: Download one of the may apps now on the market that limit your screen-time. This isn't only great for helping you switch off from work but will also help you curb your social media habit (addiction?) too. We love AppDetox and OurPact.

Why is self-control important?

Self-control and self-care often go hand in hand. Sometimes doing the best thing for our mental and physical health means saying no things. This could mean avoiding unhealthy (but admittedly fun) activities such as drinking alcohol. It's also about saying no to social engagements. Whilst a healthy social life is key to human happiness, as always, you can have too much of a good thing.

As we grow older, and friendship group expands, our social calendars can also become stretched. How many times have you looked at your diary only to realise that every weekend for the next few weeks is booked up? Between birthday parties, brunches, baby showers, and weddings, it's quite easy to say yes to everything and leave no time for yourself.

The phrase FOMO (fear of missing out) is something most people are familiar with. However, JOMO (joy f missing out) is the new trend! Try and control your urges to say yes to everything and find joy in a simple night in with your own company.

How do you take care of yourself emotionally?

Our emotions are intrinsically linked to our health and well-being, and self-care is all about being kind to yourself.

Take a moment to think about how you treat yourself when something goes wrong. This could be failing to meet a goal/ target, or making a mistake at work. A lot of us tend to have a terribly negative internal voice and beat ourselves up when things go wrong. Developing self-compassion can help you be more kind to yourself.

Think of what you would say to a good friend if he or she was facing a difficult or stressful situation. Then, when you find yourself in this kind of situation, direct these compassionate responses toward yourself.

Even if you are not facing a stressful situation, a lot of people have a demanding internal voice. This means using words such as "should," "must," and "need." Try reframing the way you speak to yourself, so you give yourself options and choice, such as, "I could do this" or "I'd like to do this because."

What role does self-care play in mental health?

Whilst self-care is important for everybody, for those that struggle with their mental health, it is absolutely paramount.

A good self-care routine can help ease symptoms of depression and anxiety. Even if you don't generally have mental health issues, a lack of self-care can result in these conditions manifesting.

If you have depression and or anxiety, self-care can help you have a healthier perspective. When we are at breaking point taking a step back to look after ourselves should be our first course of action.

Whilst a lot of self-care is individual, it's important to be open to seeking professional help when needed. Speaking to a therapist is actually part of a lot of people's self-care routine. Dedicating time to speaking about your issues, or attending courses like CBT, is important for your wellbeing, if you feel its necessary.

Self-Help Tips That Will Take You to the Next Level

Every day is rife with challenges both big and small. It's easy to get caught in a rut and keep spinning your wheels without getting anywhere. You find yourself tired, irritable, and feeling empty. You don't have the energy to do the things you love, and your bad habits seem to have multiplied faster than the clutter in your glove compartment, something has to change. Otherwise, you will become wrung out or frazzled.

When you are feeling beaten down or overwhelmed, self-help is often at the bottom of the priority list, but taking some time to focus on yourself is sometimes the best remedy for stress. Similarly, self-help is usually put on the back burner when you are flying high and filled with success, but taking care of yourself will help you stay at that high point in life for a longer period of time. So, whether you're at the end of your rope, stuck in a rut or on top of the world, here are 12 self-help tips that will take you to the next level.

Start the Morning Right

How we start our mornings has a huge impact on the rest of our day. Anyone who has had a morning go terribly wrong knows how difficult it is to get back on track in the afternoon. Imagine a morning where your alarm didn't go off, you were out of coffee, you didn't have time to shower or eat breakfast, you tripped over the cat on your way out the door, you were trapped in rush hour traffic in front of a man with road rage, and you were late to work. Now, exactly how productive do you think you would be that afternoon? The honest answer is probably "not very." Thankfully, most of us don't have to deal with many mornings that are quite that bad, but a lot of us start our day on a low note before we even get out of bed. Thousands of people sleep with their phone on their nightstand or under their pillow. The excuse is that the phone acts as an alarm, but if you keep your phone right next to the bed, you might well be scrolling through FaceBook each morning before you have stopped being horizontal.

For a productive day, start your day by saying the Serenity prayer or with a few minutes of quiet meditation instead of hunting to see who liked your Instagram post. A calmer, more focused morning will go a long way towards helping you keep your cool during the afternoon.

Get Organized

Take a look at your kitchen counter, your desk or your office. What is sitting on it? If you are like most people, you have at least one surface at home or at work where you have no idea what is piled on top of it. You also probably have clothes you never wear, extra electronics cords you never use and little odds and ends you saved "just in case." Get rid of all of them. A cluttered space is more likely to make you stressed or irritated, and the odds are you have clutter laying around because your actual storage space is filled with things you don't need. Take a rainy weekend and go through your home or office. If you find items you didn't know you had, donate them to a local Ronald McDonald's House or shelter. If you didn't know you had it, you don't need it. The same is true of clothes or "just in case" objects you haven't touched in ages. With the obvious exception of holiday decorations, get rid of anything you haven't used in the last 12 months. If you haven't used it this year, you are unlikely to need it next year.

Getting rid of clutter not only cleans your space up visually, it also removes other stresses. There are few things more frustrating than being unable to find something you really need. When you are organized, you know where you put everything. Similarly, if you get rid of the clothes you don't wear, it will be much easier to get ready in the morning.

Play

This seems like an odd piece of advice but play is important to adults as well as children. Play helps us relax and often increases our creativity. Take the time to do things you enjoy even if they don't serve an immediately apparent practical purpose. If you enjoy painting, let yourself do a watercolor piece instead of forcing yourself to channel that creativity into repainting a wall. If you like to dance, turn on some music and dance around your living room. Make it a point to do something that makes you happy every day, especially if it is something that is not "practical." Everyone needs downtime, and spending a few minutes on something you love will help you recharge and leave you better prepared to face the daily grind.

Keep Setting Goals

Everyone likes feeling accomplished or successful. Everyone also has a skill they wish to learn or improve. Put them together, and you have the importance of setting goals. Constantly setting new goals helps you keep striving for more and helps you keep the momentum generated from a success. Take a moment to think about something you would like to do or like to learn. Maybe you want to take a SCUBA diving class or pay off your debts. Write down your goal, and start working towards it. Make it a point to write down your progress or your mistakes. What gets measured is what we deem to be important. So, keep track of anything and everything that assists or prevents you from reaching your goal.

Remember Why You Started

We all have that one habit we struggle to break or that one goal we just can't seem to attain. Maybe you want to lose 10 pounds but always cave and eat the donuts your coworker buys. Maybe you always wanted to become a morning person but can't stop yourself from hitting the snooze button. For those stubborn moments of self-sabotage, think about why you started trying to break or form a habit. If you wanted to get up earlier because you have been late to work, remind yourself of that when you go to hit the snooze button in the morning. If you started dieting because you want to feel comfortable in shorts during the summer, remind yourself of that when you go to eat another slice of pizza. It takes practice to get into the habit of thinking about your "why." If reminding yourself why you started still isn't enough to break those bad habits, you might need a better "why."

Don't Take it Personally

This is so much easier said than done, but there is little that will more completely transform your life. Not taking things personally takes a lot of practice, but the reward is a life where you are no longer bothered by your snappish co-worker, by the cursing of the man with road rage behind you, or by your father-in-laws pointed remarks.

To stop taking things personally, you have to slow down. You have to learn to take advantage of the moment between when they act and when you act. That pause gives you a chance to decide if you will react or respond. If you react you are going with the knee-jerk-first-thought-in-your-head action. You take their snarky comment personally and either snarl right back or walk away from the conversation feeling attacked. If you respond, you have taken that pause and used it. You take a moment to think about why the person might have said something petty, and you remind yourself that their meanness is not about you. You let go of the how-dare-you-say-that-about-me instinct and respond with a level, calm comment. It takes a lot of practice, and you will react rather than respond when you first start, but not taking the world personally lifts a massive weight off your chest.

Take Care of Your Body

You can meditate until your legs fall off from disuse, but your mind will still be clouded and sluggish if you don't take care of your body. Now, taking care of your body doesn't mean you have to become a health guru or that you need to eat nothing but organic kale. Our bodies are evolved to be relatively low maintenance.

Taking care of your body can be an all-consuming task or an extremely minor lifestyle change, it's up to you. If you want to look like a bodybuilder or underwear model, then you will have to follow a rigid exercise routine and diet plan. If you just want your jeans to fit again, you don't have to make major changes. Drink a bare minimum of two liters of water a day and avoid heavily processed foods. You don't have to go completely all-natural or organic. Just cut back on the potato chips and store bought cookies. Also, exercise every day. It can be as simple as walking around the block when you get home from work as long as you do something every day that gets you moving.

Don't skip meals, either. Get up early enough to eat breakfast in the morning and avoid skipping lunch. If you miss a meal, you are far more likely to make poor food choices later in the day. If you are never hungry in the morning, you don't have to eat a huge breakfast but have at least a banana to give your body the fuel it needs.

Find a Spiritual Connection

Connecting to the wider world brings a sense of peace to your life and forces you to slow down for at least a few minutes. Whether you start a Bible study, attend a synagogue, or join a local coven, tapping into your spiritual side gives you a unique boost of energy. Most people who start regularly putting time into some sort of spiritual or religious development find an increased sense of purpose, strength, motivation, and peace in their lives. Churches, mosques, and temples are also a great way to meet people who share similar values.

Give Back

Giving back to your community will help you feel like you are making a difference in the world. People tend to derive a great deal of satisfaction from helping others, and working with the less fortunate individuals in your area can help you appreciate what you have.

Volunteer opportunities are available beyond traditional soup kitchens as well. Animal shelters are almost always in need of volunteers, and organizations like Big Brothers, Big Sisters or events like Relay for Life rely on volunteers. Take the time to find a cause you are passionate about and donate some of your time. Organize a K9's For Warriors color run or a community yard sale that donates its proceeds to St. Jude. Donating time, instead of money, lets you truly connect to the cause you are supporting, meet people who share your passion and lets you see how you are making at least a small difference in the world.

Be Grateful

Scientists have proven that it is impossible to be grateful and stressed at the same time. The odds are good that you have a lot that is causing you stress but also many reasons to feel gratitude. Take some time every day to think about the reasons you have to be grateful. Keep a gratitude journal and list all the reasons you have to be grateful before you go to bed. List five things you are grateful for at lunch or as you make coffee in the morning, and yes, coffee can be one of those things.

Gratitude has an interesting snowball effect. The more you focus on what you are grateful for, the more reasons you find to show gratitude. This cycle builds to keep you in a grateful state of mind all day and helps combat depression and anxiety better than simple optimism.

Sleep

It's extraordinary how often this is forgotten. Starting as young as middle school, we find ourselves in a self-destructive competition to see who got the least amount of sleep. This awful contest continues into the adult world where sleep deprivation is equated to work ethic. In reality, however, losing sleep doesn't mean you are working harder. It means you are destroying your mind and body. Seven to nine hours of sleep is essential to keep both the mind and the body in working order. If you've ever spent a week skimping on sleep, you probably remember having little energy, being unable to focus and eating poorly. You also might not remember much of that week at all, because while we are sleeping, our brain is hard at work storing our memories. If you don't sleep, you don't remember. It's that simple. Sleep is also when our bodies flush naturally occurring toxins from our brains. If you miss enough sleep, you can start suffering from brain inflammation.

Very few people are willing to form good sleeping habits despite their simplicity. If you want a good night's sleep, turn off your electronics at least 30 minutes before bed and read a book. The bright light of a screen keeps your body from producing melatonin, an essential hormone for sleep. Reading a book, however, involves lower light and makes your eyes tired. Tired eyes trick your brain into thinking you are sleepier than you actually are and helps you fall asleep faster. For long term sleep health, develop a bedtime routine and turn the lights out at a similar time each night. Your body will fall into a rhythm that makes it easier to go to bed at night and get up in the morning feeling rested.

Self-help doesn't have to involve a massive overhaul of your life. A change as small as going to bed 15 minutes earlier can make a world of difference. Think about what you want to change and develop a plan to break or make that habit. Then, stick to it. Taking it to the next level is that hard and that simple at the same time.

CHAPTER FIVE

BUILD UP YOUR SELF-ESTEEM

Self-esteem is usually thought as a subjective appraisal of one's self. It is generally believed that self-esteem is nothing but your own opinion of yourself. It is not something outside of you, but something internal. Self-esteem is about how we feel on the inside, and such feeling will affect how we act on outside. Our self-esteem helps to determine our personality and shapes our character, decides how we react to the experiences and challenges we face in our lives and certainly affect our interaction with other people too. Living in a healthy environment for a pretty long period, positive thinking, constructive efforts, and feel-good activities enhance not only ones confidence and learning, but also provide us a strong base for our future goals and achievements. So, one can easily deal with obstacles with courage required and maintain high level of self-esteem. As a result, the level of satisfaction and esteem would be so high that to achieve lofty aims such as self-actualization, self-enhancement, and the level of 'ideal' self.

Self-esteem is not an independent concept; it is intermixed with other significant concepts like self-respect, self-pride, self-confidence, self-dignity, etc. All these concepts could never be separated from self-esteem. Like when we are capable of writing alphabets, able of reading alphabets, of joining them together in a meaningful sentence so that we could understand what it means. We can finally say that we can read and write in English to some extent or to some level. Likewise when we are capable of making decisions, when we achieve some goals based on our confidence and efforts, when we are being appreciated by the people we consider important, we earn some good position in our society, we feel we are respectable human beings. Such feelings ultimately lead us toward high self-esteem. In other words, we are enjoying/gaining a higher level of self-esteem.

In this chapter, we focus on the environmental factors affecting ones self-esteem tremendously. Although to change ones environment is a next to impossible task, it is fact that if we go into a different situation or we change our situation temporarily, we feel different. When we are in the company of strangers, we feel scared/composed, and when we are in the company of friends, we feel secure and happy. We can choose a better company very easily. In the same way, when we set attainable goals and achieve them at last, we feel confident and successful, conversely, if we choose goals that we could not achieve by some way or the other, we feel discouraged, low and segregated. Here it could be wisely said that we should choose our goals intelligently and carefully. In short, the crux of the discussion is that whether it is matter of choosing friends or setting goals, we can try our best to change our present situation to raise our self-esteem.

Now the question is why to change our environment? After all, we can change our thinking and feelings only to get higher self-esteem. In fact, only changing our thinking and feeling cannot solve our problem at all. We need to do something else that would be considered as a significant change in our environment, otherwise our overall self-esteem would never be so high to protect us. The more change (good or positive) in our environment, the more our self-esteem would be.

The environmental factors that could be changed by human energy can also be discussed separately. Such as status (marital, educational, professional, social, health, financial), place of living, clothing or dressing style, people we met or communicate with, tasks we love to perform, and being positive would be thought as the critical/basic levels of change.

Hierarchically, in the process of change, the most important factor is 'finance' by which you would be able to change your place, company, and tasks easily. It is the basics of all changes you could think and implement. So, in this chain of steps, being financially strong (to its basic level) is the first step, and then come other steps to follow. However, without being financially strong, you could find other ways to change your environment but this process is very tricky and time consuming.

In the second stage of change, if you are capable of earning good money already, you must strive for a good place where you can not only live comfortably rather have interaction with people whom you like and who like you and where you could also achieve more success and set new goals to achieve more confidence and resilience as well. In other words, in this stage, while having enough money, proper place (in terms of weather conditions, facilities, beauty) and high status, if you don't have good friends, you would need to change that place too to have new friends who could appreciate/encourage you and enhance your self-esteem. Naturally, you would enhance their self-esteem too in return. This interaction is most important otherwise we would never be satisfied with ourselves and with others. Here it is important to argue that good friends can also be found while living at the same place if we try our best but in most of the cases it is next to impossible due to different limitations present around us. Under extreme limitations, temporary replacement of living could also solve the problem.

After having a change in our social surroundings, the most powerful feelings we would need is 'to be loved' or to be with loving people in our circles where we move. It's true that everybody has loving families to take care of them, but after certain age when we need independence, liberty, and status. We need others (not immediate relatives) who could appreciate us, recognize our efforts, and value them to enhance our self-esteem. Those "others" could be anybody, among our friends/colleagues or just outsiders whose names we sometimes even don't remember. In the new environment, there are ample chances to find some 'others' more appreciating and loving than we have presently. Even if we don't find our desired social circle, we should not become desperate and keep on moving until or unless we find it as we deserve.

In the third stage of change, if we have first three things (good income, good place, and good company), and don't have any desired goal to achieve in our life, we will also feel unsatisfied, uncomfortable, empty, dull and bored. Since there is no improvement in our learning status, we would never be happy by pretending/appreciating remarks of our friends/colleagues. Lastly, these three factors/things would provide us the basics of our self-satisfaction and are essentials to our self-esteem.

Although it looks ridiculous to take a step to change our environment, it is reality that sometimes, things we need (loving, friendly, and accepting people, good weather, new opportunities, rising status, higher income, etc.), can only be dramatically and easily achieved by changing the environment, especially the place with different culture (most suitable environment for you). It is the most important step toward high self-esteem and of course it will bring more rapid and expected results as well. Other changes/benefits related to your social status enhancement and self-satisfaction would follow this action and reactions of the particular environment would decide your behavior in turn, which would lead you towards higher self-esteem that is your ultimate goal.

Here it is very essential to mention that such decisions would require a deep understanding of our nature too. There are people who never consider it important to change a place to get an adjustment rather they are very contented and satisfied with the position they have. Such persons need no change and may need something else to uplift their self-esteem (to discuss such needs is out of scope of this chapter). But for most of us, we don't recognize what is our basic problem; we need a change, not in our thinking, but rather in our environment. We need better 'others' to provide us positive feedback, to make us happy and satisfied in a way we wish. Such change is not very easy to manipulate, but it would need a lot of courage and decision power. Realistically it would need us to be financially strong enough to take measures accordingly as well as being mentally fit/strong enough to make decisions of our choice.

In rare circumstances, due to our specific limitations, if we can't change our location as well as our fellow beings, it would be strongly suggested to better change our attitude or behavior (not thinking or beliefs). Although it is very easy to say to change ourself, but it is the most difficult task in our journey to achieve high self-esteem, especially with adults. Unfortunately, there isn't enough literature, movies or plays for our youngsters to follow good roles in their lives about how to react to negative remarks/attitudes of others. Rather, habits that are typical to low esteemed people are very much prevalent and appreciated and those with high esteemed people are mostly neglected and uncommon. That is why change in self-esteem for adults becomes a challenge.

Realistically speaking, after achieving goals described above, we need to practice more on how to get and maintain higher and higher self-esteem under present environmental factors. We need to know that in case, something desired/required could not be achieved/changed, how this problem should be tackled to protect our self-esteem. There is a vast literature available in the books of self-esteem everywhere in the world that will provide us the rules of thinking and enhancing our self-esteem by just putting efforts at our level best.

We also need to develop new ideas/concepts/beliefs based on which we could set TV serials or school curriculum to teach our children about how to deal with self-esteem issues. In this way, they could learn how to enhance self-esteem in its real sense to guide them throughout their life and even modify their environment instead of letting environment change/raise their self-esteem. Additionally there should be very specific examples of events from our daily life in the curriculum of children, which cause low self-esteem among people or children, and then there must be specific solutions to that. Otherwise only books or teaching material on raising self-esteem would never be the solution of the problem.

Indeed every new adjustment in life is a crisis in self-esteem and as a result, we, as human beings, by nature, always strive for good/positive self-esteem. It is just like a war; a war between our true self, expected self and interpretations of our environmental experiences. It is a kind of a continuous struggle that would never end and will always push us towards higher and higher self-esteem (provided we acknowledge it as a positive phenomenon of nature) until the time of death.

Healthy Self-esteem

How we feel about ourselves is one of the key factors in how happy our life feels to us. A healthy sense of self drives our dreams, defines our relationships, and allows for more balanced and resilient emotional states. It is essential and yet for many, it feels not just elusive but unimaginable.

When low self-esteem exists, it is often so pervasive; seeping into every aspect of one's life, it makes it easy to assume that most people feel the feelings they struggle with. I have noted that when clients come to work on self-esteem, there is an underlying belief that only those with outstanding external successes or extreme physical attributes or talents have healthy self-acceptance. This is not true and often even in those cases, the people we note as "worthy" or having achieved healthy self-esteem, may also be struggling in spite of what we see externally.

So how does healthy self-esteem feel? What does it look like? When a person feels a healthy sense of self-esteem, they are not effected deeply by disapproval or criticism of others. A person with healthy self-esteem measure other peoples feedback in light of their own internal beliefs and feelings. This means they can hear others without feeling they are worthless, or diminished by the beliefs of others.

Along those same lines, they don't feel the need to defend themselves to others, or blame others for mistakes or shortcomings. Those with healthy self-esteem are likely to be externally successful however their achievements are not fueled by a need to prove themselves as much as a sense of meaning and purpose. There is a sense of deep peace and personal power that comes with healthy self-esteem; an acceptance that perfection does not need to exist or constant approval of others to feel safe in one's life and a deep and abiding belief that one can change themselves and their life if they so desire.

There was an excitement about popularized psychology in the 60s and 70s. Everyday people were reading about important topics like self-esteem in books like "I'm OK; You're OK." One would think all these decades later, the availability of self-improvement resources would have caused an increase in the number of people with healthy self-esteem. Still, this seems to not be the case. More than ever, subsequent generations have been struggling with self-esteem in spite of the influx of information. So, why is this the case and how does one acquire a healthy sense of self?

The answer lies in a balanced definition and understanding of the topic. Self-esteem is a core belief about oneself, an attitude about oneself as worthy or unworthy of happiness and one's being capable of meeting life's challenges. These two things need to be in balance in order to have healthy self-esteem. In some ways, it can be said that the information of the previous decades went wrong in terms of what was emphasized.

When people begin to think of self-esteem only in terms of having good feelings about oneself, it is similar to having many blank checks and no money in the bank to back it up. Noted, psychotherapist Nathaniel Branden, Ph.D.'s definition of self-esteem reflects balanced thinking when he defines self-esteem as; "The experience of being capable of meeting life's challenges and being worthy of happiness." The competence aspect of self-esteem balances the worthiness aspect and is developed through realistic and accurate appraisals of oneself, the ability to overcome adversity, the ability to take reasonable pride in one's accomplishments, and spring back from failures.

When a person focuses only on good feelings about oneself then they may have a false sense of esteem that only remains intact if others around them reinforce their good feelings. Many parents trying to create good self-esteem in their children, lavished them with praise in all situations, even when the attributes or performance were not grounded in reality as being praiseworthy. Practices like giving every participant a trophy for example can create an inflated sense of self-efficacy. This makes for a lot of unhappiness and feeling the need to defend oneself to maintain feeling good, which is an exhausting and unsatisfying way to live. False and low self-esteem also creates a host of other potential issues such as limiting experiences of living, not pursuing dreams and goals, and also gravitating to unhealthy relationships.

If you want to begin building your self-esteem here are a few beginning steps.

1. The first step is being honest with yourself, because often this is an issue. It will be the first step to empowering you to change.

2. Don't allow yourself to remain in a state of blaming others for this state. Although parents and family of origin may have been factors in low self-esteem, they too likely struggled with the same issues and didn't mean to pass them on to you. When a person stays in a state of blaming others, it is a trap that keeps one stuck.

3. Stop all negative self-talk. This is a process of retraining yourself. Begin with recognizing when it occurs, interrupt the thought and choose a kinder thought to say to yourself. You may also consider hypnosis for help with this issue. Reoccurring thoughts can be directly challenged through hypnosis and the overall sense of harsh self-judgment can be shifted to a more healthy self-acceptance.

4. Stop comparing yourself and your life to others to judge worthiness or unworthiness. There are always people who have more or less than you of something. This has little to do with their worthiness or yours and it distracts from the real issue, which exists in you, not external to you. Comparing to others is a waste of energy that will just leave you feeling bad and stuck.

5. Begin to work with a counselor who can help you challenge the other issues associated with low self-esteem, such as the balanced healthy viewpoint of oneself, setting healthy boundaries with others, and building personal competencies. All of these areas of development are well worth the time and effort they take.

Increase Your Self Esteem

There are many people who do not have good self-esteem. This is unfortunate because self-esteem can be such a powerful motivator. If a person has good self-esteem, he or she will have enough confidence to try things out of their comfort zone and turn their dreams into reality. Unfortunately, most people with low self-esteem have been knocked down so many times before in the past that they just don't want to get hurt anymore. Even though it may hurt, it is important to increase your self-esteem so you can live a more fulfilling life. So, how long does it take to increase your self-esteem?

The answer to this question really just depends on the person. The amount of time it will take you to increase your self-esteem is contingent on a few factors. One of the main factors is willingness. If you are really willing to increase your self-esteem, you will be able to do it in a much shorter period of time. If you are increasing your self-esteem because somebody else wants you to, it will be harder to do and take more time. It is important to remember that you should only raise your self-esteem if it is something that you want to do.

Another factor that will determine how long it will take you to increase your self-esteem is your past. If your self-esteem was severely damaged in the past, it will take you a lot longer to forgive yourself and move on. For most people, forgiving themselves for letting other people damage their confidence is the hardest part of the process. Once you have forgiven yourself, the rebuilding can start to happen.

Age is a factor that many people do not think of. The reason age can play a role in the amount of time it takes a person to increase their self-esteem is because people who are older realize they do not have as much time left to live. Because of this, older people generally speed the process up because they want to live as much of their life as possible with a higher self-esteem. Younger people realize they have more time to live, so they are able to really focus on the root of the problem.

Gender can play a role in how much time it takes for a person to increase their self-esteem. For the most part, women tend to spend more time on the healing process than men. In the end, this might be beneficial for women because they usually increase their self-esteem. For men who rush the problem, there could be problems in the future because the base of the problem didn't get solved.

Obviously, the personality type of the individual will have a big influence on the amount of time it takes for the person to increase his or her self-esteem. People with aggressive personalities tend to increase their self-esteem faster than people with passive personalities.

If you want to fix your self-esteem problem once and for all, it is important that you do not rush the process. Even though you want to heal and forget about what happened in your past, it is very important to flush it out of your system first. This usually requires going back through the events in detail and figuring out what went wrong. After you have learned from the past, you can forget about it. Many people have the tendency to either not think about their past or not truly find out why their self-esteem was so low. If you feel like this is happening to you at anytime during the healing process, it is best to start over.

Since you now know that the amount of time it takes to increase a person's self-esteem depends on many different factors, remember to take your time and do it right the first time. It is better to take a year to properly increase your self-esteem than to do it in a month but the wrong way. If you increase your self-esteem properly the first time, you will feel much better in the end. People who try to rush the process the first time and end up failing tend to take another blow in the self-esteem level, which could end up being detrimental. Once you have increased your self-esteem, you will feel so much better about yourself. Everything in life will seem so much easier and enjoyable. You are definitely making the right choice by attempting to increase your self-esteem. If you put in enough effort and take your time, you will accomplish your goal in no time.

Steps to an Improved Self-Esteem

How many good qualities did you discover in yourself? Your self-confidence is good when there are more positive qualities than negative and poor when the number of negative characteristics is bigger than the positive. But it is also important for good self-esteem to notice the weaknesses and be honest about them.

You can guard yourself with good self-esteem

Do you believe in yourself and appreciate yourself? Self-esteem can also be defined as self-worth, or it can be described as the quantity of self-esteem and self-confidence. Self-worth is that you defend yourself, keep up your rights and are capable to be satisfied with your performance. Self-confidence is how much you think you can impact your life with your own abilities and solutions, and how you can deal future concerns and problems. Self-confidence is that you dare to set high standards and take on challenges.

You respect yourself enough to hold your rights

Do you see your own life as a unique and important? Good self-esteem is that you can see the uniqueness of your own life and understand that you are important, without that it has to be pointed out to you by special achievements or successes. Self-esteem is a sense inside of you - it cannot be explained through the things that you can see from the outside.

Valuing others is a component of good self-esteem

Are you able to value other individuals? Piece of good self-esteem is the skill to appreciate other people's views, skills and pay respect and recognition to him or her. A person who has a strong self-esteem, is capable to see their own worth and competence, but he does not think he is the only one who knows how to, or the only one that will be appreciated.

Are you independent in your own solutions and independent of other individual's opinions? A someone who has a strong self-esteem, do not have to constantly think about what other people think and he does not always try to think and act in favor to public judgment. This courage is independence in the sense that you dare to make your own decisions and have your own opinions and live the life in the way you want and not in the way what your surroundings value or appreciate.

Good self-esteem is the ability to put up with disappointments

Are you able to deal with failures and disappointments? Good self-esteem is also the ability to put up with disappointments and failures. Good self-esteem eases the granting your own mistakes, the fact that you did some task poorly, does not mean you are not good. The granting of a failure provides a chance to consider what you could learn from the matter, so that the new failure could be avoided. Good self-esteem helps us to realize there are disappointments in every people's lives, even though they are not always displayed on the outside.

What self-esteem is not?

Self-esteem is not the equal as performing confidently or outside success. Self-esteem is not just self-confidence and seeing yourself only in a positive manner. Self-esteem is not social courage or selfishness. No one can have just plain poor self-esteem or a complete self-confidence. You should not even try to achieve complete self-confidence, because it is no longer human or achievable.

No one can have a complete self-confidence

Everyone's self-esteem is good in some area and then a little worse in another. If a person takes on a role and discovers that he can behave as if he were truly like his role, this sooner or later starts to impact his or her self-image. Even though an adult's self-image is usually already settled, there are a few ways you can build yourself a better self-esteem.

Five steps to better self-esteem.

1. Highlight the success in your own head.

2. Find positive and valuable things in your life.

3. Be fearless and take more difficult tasks that you think you could do.

4. Remember in "the universe of super-achievers," you have the right to be in doubt and a little bit worried about your survival.

5. Hold in mind high self-esteem is not a guarantee of satisfaction and a good life, or the lack of it does not forecast a poor life

Good self-esteem makes life easier, but low self-esteem is not a disaster.

CHAPTER SIX

YOU OWE YOURSELF AN APOLOGY

An apology is a statement that has two key elements:

1. It shows your remorse over your actions.

2. It acknowledges the hurt that your actions have caused to someone else.

We all need to learn how to apologize, after all, no one is perfect. We all make mistakes, and we all have the capability to hurt people through our behaviors and actions, whether these are intentional or not.

It isn't always easy to apologize, but it's the most effective way to restore trust and balance in a relationship, when you've done something wrong.

Why Apologize?

To Yourself -

Why? Because you have been mistreating yourself since you were in elementary school. You have allowed outsiders to tell you who you are and what you are worth. Then, you internalized all of the negative talk and kicked it into high gear by telling yourself things such as, "I'm stupid. I'm ugly" You pick yourself apart for every little flaw and imperfection you have. It plays in your subconscious mind like an endless looping tape. This is causing your body to respond to the negativity, negatively. Why should anyone else give you respect and honor you deserve if you do not afford your own self with dignity? STOP IT! You deserve better, even from you!

To others -

There are many reasons why you should make a sincere apology when you've hurt someone unnecessarily, or have made a mistake.

First, an apology opens a dialogue between yourself and the other person. Your willingness to admit your mistake can give the other person the opportunity he needs to communicate with you, and start dealing with his feelings.

When you apologize, you also acknowledge that you engaged in unacceptable behavior. This helps you rebuild trust and reestablish your relationship with the other person. It also gives you a chance to discuss what is and isn't acceptable.

What's more, when you admit that the situation was your fault, you restore dignity to the person you hurt. This can begin the healing process, and it can ensure that she doesn't unjustly blame herself for what happened.

Last, a sincere apology shows that you're taking responsibility for your actions. This can strengthen your self-confidence, self-respect, and reputation. You're also likely to feel a sense of relief when you come clean about your actions, and it's one of the best ways to restore your integrity in the eyes of others.

Consequences of Not Apologizing

What are the consequences if you don't apologize when you've made a mistake?

First, you will damage your relationships with colleagues, clients, friends, or family. It can harm your reputation, limit your career opportunities, and lower your effectiveness, and, others may not want to work with you.

It also negatively affects your team when you don't apologize. No one wants to work for a boss who can't own up to his mistakes, and who doesn't apologize for them. The animosity, tension, and pain that comes with this can create a toxic work environment.

Why Apologies Are Difficult

With all these negative consequences, why do some people still refuse to apologize?

First, apologies take courage. When you admit you were wrong, it puts you in a vulnerable position, which can open you up to attack or blame. Some people struggle to show this courage.

Alternatively, you may be so full of shame and embarrassment over your actions that you can't bring yourself to face the other person.

Or, you may be following the advice "never apologize, never explain." It's up to you if you want to be this arrogant, but, if you do, don't expect to be seen as a wise or an inspiring leader.

How to Apologize Appropriately

Step 1: Express Remorse

Every apology needs to start with two magic words, "I'm sorry," or "I apologize." This is essential because these words express remorse over your actions.

For example, you could say, "I'm sorry that I snapped at you yesterday. I feel embarrassed and ashamed by the way I acted."

Your words need to be sincere and authentic. Be honest with yourself, and with the other person, about why you want to apologize. Never make an apology when you have ulterior motives, or if you see it as a means to an end.

Timeliness is also important here. Apologize as soon as you realize that you've wronged someone else.

Step 2: Admit Responsibility

Next, admit responsibility for your actions or behavior, and acknowledge what you did.

Here, you need to empathize with the person you wronged, and demonstrate that you understand how you made her feel.

Don't make assumptions, instead, simply try to put yourself in that person's shoes and imagine how she felt.

For example, "I know that I hurt your feelings yesterday when I snapped at you. I'm sure this embarrassed you, especially since everyone else on the team was there. I was wrong to treat you like that."

Step 3: Make Amends

When you make amends, you take action to make the situation right.

Here are two examples:

- "If there's anything that I can do to make this up to you, please just ask."
- "I realize that I was wrong to doubt your ability to chair our staff meeting. I'd like you to lead the team through tomorrow's meeting to demonstrate your skills."

Think carefully about this step. Token gestures or empty promises will do more harm than good. Because you feel guilty, you might also be tempted to give more than what's appropriate, so be proportionate in what you offer.

Step 4: Promise That It Won't Happen Again

Your last step is to explain that you won't repeat the action or behavior.

This step is important because you reassure the other person that you're going to change your behavior. This helps you rebuild trust and repair the relationship.

You could say, "From now on, I'm going to manage my stress better, so that I don't snap at you and the rest of the team. And, I want you to call me out if I do this again."

Make sure that you honor this commitment in the days or weeks to come. If you promise to change your behavior, but don't follow through, others will question your reputation and your trustworthiness.

CHAPTER SEVEN

DEFEATING THE ENEMY INSIDE OF YOU

Every day is a battle against the enemy within that never leaves your side.

This enemy is relentless and unforgiving.

Your biggest enemy in the world is yourself. It's the inner voice of doubt in your head that tells you you're insignificant.

You're currently losing if you say things like:

"I'm not good enough."

"I suck."

"I don't deserve this."

"I'll never be able to do that."

"I can't."

Picture that inner voice as a wrecking crew, demolishing any ounce of happiness you deserve. The enemy within is a wrecking ball with the sole purpose to tear you down slowly from the inside.

You must take back your mind but you're letting the negative voice reign victorious while your positive voice curls under a rock in defeat. With a crushed spirit, it's easier to wave the white flag and surrender.

You're a loser and you don't deserve to win, right?

The more you keep wasting your time, energy and thoughts on telling yourself you're not good enough, the more you will continue to be right. You will destroy your future happiness.

I write this to desperately convince you that you deserve to be happy and deserve to win.

I want to teach you how to fight the enemy within because I've been slowly winning the battle in my own head.

You have to find ways to feel good about yourself. You have to will your way to smaller victories so you can gain confidence and momentum.

Here are 4 ways to fight back and dismantle the wrecking ball. It's time to start winning and take your life back.

1. Fuel Your Mind for Battle

To conquer that inner voice of doubt, you need to equip yourself with the necessary weapons to defend against the enemy within.

If you're having a hard time believing in yourself, I'd like to ask what you consume on a daily basis?

You become what you consume so you must be mindful of what you let in your mind.

If you're wasting your time feeding your brain endless hours of Netflix, YouTube videos, and video games, you're going to have a hard time pulling yourself out of this hole. You have nothing positive to draw motivation from, you have no line of defense.

On the flip side, consuming personal development material and positive content will fuel your mind and prepare you for victory.

I noticed a massive improvement in my life when I cut out the garbage and starting gorging on personal development content. I've become obsessed with books, audio books, and podcasts. Not only do they provide me with the uplift I need to defend my mind, but they also give me a ton of ideas that I source for drawings and writing.

Applying these teachings and talking to yourself will help you dismantle that wrecking ball quite quickly.

2. Get Crazy, Talk to Yourself

That inner voice is going to bombard you with relentless blows to your confidence, trying to convince you that you're not good enough and that you don't deserve happiness.

This is when you counterpunch with positive, affirming self-talk.

It may sound weird and uncomfortable, but you need to start talking to yourself. Look yourself in the eyes and start saying:

"Why not me?"

"Why can't I?"

"I deserve this."

"I can and I will."

"I will be great."

When you tell yourself these things each day, you will slowly start to regain control. These are small daily victories which build momentum.

I talk to myself every day. It was extremely uncomfortable at first but now it's empowering. When I start to feel down on myself, I am able to talk myself out of it.

3. Get Your Body Right

Many times we lose the daily battles because we are ashamed of our physical appearance.

I hit rock bottom when I was overweight, drinking every day and couldn't get a job within my field of expertise. I couldn't get my mind right because I couldn't get past how disgusting I felt I looked.

When you start taking care of yourself by exercising and dieting, you begin to like the way you feel and how you begin to look.

When you look good, you feel good. When you feel good, you play good. Life is a sport and we are just playing the game.

It's important to feel good about yourself. What's great about the gym is that you release endorphins, making you feel on top of the world after a workout. Sure, you will go through a little pain but pain is temporary and you leave with another small victory.

A small amount of pain for a lifetime of happiness is always a solid trade off.

Getting your physical self right is like bringing in reinforcements as you wage war on the enemy within.

4. Treat Failure Like Progress

Something that holds us back from getting what we deserve is fear. It's a tactic the enemy within implements to paralyze you from challenging the status quo and taking action.

You passively exist due to the fear of failing, being ridiculed, or looking stupid in front of people. However, true failure results from quitting or never trying in the first place.

Failing is a part of my everyday routine. I fail so much and I use this to my advantage as I discover something that didn't work, which gets me closer to the thing that will work.

Failure is measurable progress and funnels you down a path to success by showing you the areas which need improvement.

This is called failing forward and is only possible by confronting your fears and being prepared to fail. Failing is essential to become successful.

Destroy the enemy within

When you conquer the enemy within, no enemy outside can do you harm.

Stop wasting your energy and invest in yourself. You'll never get to where you want to be by tearing yourself down.

I challenge you this week to get out of your comfort zone and start talking to yourself at least once a day. Tell yourself you deserve to be happy and that you are capable. I guarantee by the end of the week you will start believing yourself more and more.

How badly do you want to be happy?

- Your biggest enemy in the world is yourself
- You become what you consume
- Consuming personal development material will help you dismantle the wrecking crew
- Counterpunch the inner voice of doubt with positive, affirming self-talk
- It's important to feel good about yourself
- True failure results from never trying or quitting when something didn't work
- Failure is measurable progress
- When you conquer the enemy within, no enemy outside can do you no harm

Two sides of the same coin

Your perceived self is the self that needs most loving yet a lot of people disregard themselves every day, instead choosing to love their ideal self.

Imagine if you have two children, one of them is hard work and you seem to be constantly on at them for one reason or another, and the other is nearly perfect and you never have to tell them off for any reason. Would you love the 'hard work' child any less than the 'perfect child?' Of course you wouldn't. It just means you have to find a way to work better with the 'hard work' child and gently coax them and encourage them.

So it is with your perceived self. You should look for ways to work better with your perceived self and accept yourself for who are are at the moment, knowing that change will come through gentle coaxing and encouragement and not forever declaring war with yourself.

Steps to accepting your perceived self

1. Acknowledge it

If there's something you don't like about yourself, acknowledge it. For example, I acknowledge the fact my stomach is slightly protruding.

- Accept it.

    You don't have to like it but accept the fact, for the moment, that you have something you dislike about yourself.

- Thank yourself.

    To acknowledge and accept something about yourself that you are not happy with takes guts and honesty. Thank yourself for that.

- Know why you want change.

If you want change to happen, know exactly why you want the change. Get right down to the core of 'why.' For example, I want to change my protruding stomach so my husband still finds me attractive. Why? So, I can be accepted by my husband. Why? So I can have a deep relationship. Why? So I can feel content. Why? You get the picture, just get deep down to the root of why you want to change.

- Gentle change as opposed to drastic change.

  Gently coaxing yourself to change helps you to feel less stressed. If you want to lose weight keep eating the cheeseburgers for now but coax yourself to go to the gym or go for a walk after or before. You will find by doing this, change will happen more naturally and the momentum will build up into the change you want.

The cycle of change

All change has a cycle to it whatever it is, from drug addiction to learning to read. The model from Prochaska and DiClemente states there are 5 stages to change:

1. Pre-contemplative

You're happy munching the cheeseburgers and don't really care about your weight. and are not thinking about doing anything to change

- Contemplative

  You think maybe you are eating too many cheeseburgers and maybe need to do something about your weight.

- Action

  When you have actually managed to join the gym and start attending whilst cutting down on the cheeseburgers.

- Maintenance

    This is when you maintain your momentum and you keep going to the gym and are beginning to see change happen.

- Relapse

    The stage where you have not been to the gym for a few weeks and munch on a few more cheeseburgers than you did at the action/eminence stage.

All of the stages serve their purpose and all of the stages will happen throughout the cycle of any change. So, just because you relapse doesn't mean you are never going to change, it just means you need to learn some more and the relapse will help with this.

The way others see you

It's important to say that your perceived self is not necessarily the way others see you, however the way others see you is not going to help you in your war between your perceived self and your ideal self. No matter how many times someone tells you that you are good at something if you believe you are not good at it nothing anybody says will change you. You are the only person to be able to change you.

Sometimes drastic intervention is required by other people when you might have an overly distorted self image, such as people with anorexia. This is a mental health issue and should be treated professionally. However, for the most part we all have a pretty accurate self-image.

Don't be too hard on yourself

Most people want to change something about themselves, even Brad Pitt and Beyonce', we are all in the same boat. You want what they have and they want what you have. Accept yourself for who you are but acknowledge that you want to change, if you really do, and gently coax yourself. Then there will be peace between the perceived self and the ideal self.

CHAPTER EIGHT

AVOID LOSING YOUR CORE IDENTITY

What's Your Identity?

So what exactly is your "identity," anyway? Simply put, it's the facets of your life which define your roles, or describe what's important to you. It's the "structure" of the "inner" you. Consider this example:

> The "you" at the core has roles, beliefs, interests and natural traits. The closer the concept to your core, the more heavily it contributes to who you are. Solid lines here indicate strength of the concept to your identity. Healthy individuals have well-defined components. Those can change during a lifetime, but it is usually due to life events. Experience, developing new interests, new perspectives, changing roles in life are typically how our identity evolves over time. Changes don't happen overnight, they generally change gradually as we continue to grow in life.

"Me" Becomes "We"

Entering into a new relationship can be thrilling and give us an emotionally "full" feeling. All the hormonal effects that come with that feeling of euphoria can make us feel like we're fulfilled and complete. That satisfaction can consume our attention, leaving our other interests hanging. As the relationship grows, both people's identity components come back into play to one degree or another, creating a pair of two "whole," but integrated people.

Sometimes it doesn't happen like that. As it grows, it's possible for a partner's identity to get "absorbed" or suppressed by the other. How do you know if you've lost your identity?

Signs to Watch For:

You've stopped seeing friends: In our example, you might be a "helpful friend" at your core. A change in your identity can be seen when you're directing all that "helpfulness" toward your partner and your attention toward your friends seems to disappear. It is common for friends to see less of each other as life's demands increase, but when your reasons for losing touch seems to be focused like a laser at your partner, you might be losing your identity.

You've stopped your individual hobbies: It's normal for people to get distracted from doing things they enjoy. Usually, we keep those in the back of our minds and recognize it as something to get back to when time allows because it's inherently satisfying. Our partners support and encourage us to do these things because they make us happy. In our example, "dancing" is becoming weakened or shaky due to the other person's preference, not yours. If you find yourself neglecting enjoyable hobbies because your partner doesn't enjoy it or doesn't approve, and it feels like a loss, you might be losing your identity.

Your interests/values are replaced with your partner's: It's normal and healthy to share interests and values, having those in common probably brought you together. It's also okay to change your perspective based on experience, but when you find yourself changing your viewpoints to be more compatible with your partner, you might be losing your identity.

You're doing things to please your partner that don't make you happy: We all do things to make our partners happy. It's part of the give-and-take of a relationship. Sometimes, though, our instinct tells us what we're doing is wrong, or we are extremely uncomfortable. If you ignore that gut sense and do it anyway, you are one step closer to losing your identity each time you do it.

You're preoccupied with how your partner would react to…: Being concerned with how your loved one would feel about things is good. Empathy and sensitivity are good, and treating others with those is very good. But when you find yourself basing most of your reactions, interactions, and decisions on what the other person would likely approve of, you are probably losing your identity.

How To Get Yourself Back

Reconnect with other people important to you: Schedule in time with friends or family. These people were important to you before for a reason. Go for walks, have dinner, do what you love with those people. Be sure to carve out time, don't see if you can "fit it in" around everything else you and your partner are doing.

Pick your hobbies back up: Doing things that satisfy and nurture you are important in keeping mentally and physically healthy. Staying true to what "feeds" you is part of what made you yourself. If your partner is open to trying it with you, then great. If not, do it anyway. You deserve it.

Set boundaries: Having your own time, activities, or "space" (however that looks for you), are normal and healthy in a relationship. This doesn't mean you're shutting your partner out. There are lines, and then there are walls. Define the lines that make you most comfortable.

Pursue your dreams: If finishing that degree was always your plan but got lost, what got in your way? Sometimes we have to postpone things because other things are pressing, but if it's important enough, we'll get back on track. Going for our passions energizes and propels us to better things. Your vision for your future is yours, and in a healthy relationship, there's room for your "full" self and a partner. How to Regain Your Self-Respect Once It's Lost

Many people don't think about self-respect until they realize they've lost it.

By then, however, it can be very difficult to find the courage to rebuild what's gone. While it isn't impossible to regain self-respect, it does take a great deal of effort and determination.

Yet, how can you learn to respect yourself, especially when you don't currently feel any such regard? Here are some tips to respect yourself, rebuild or regain self-respect, and keep it.

Know that you can rebuild

With self-respect such a crucial component of overall well-being, knowing that you can rebuild it once you've lost it is very important. You must believe that this is so. Otherwise, you'll forever hate yourself. What's vital in this rebuilding process is to maintain an optimistic attitude toward your efforts and make a point of working diligently at it.

Accept your mistakes and pledge to do better

Everyone makes mistakes. Mistakes only chip away at your self-esteem if you continue to beat yourself up over them. Accept that you've erred, pledge to do better, and make good on the commitment.

Stop worrying what other people think and stay true to your core values and beliefs

There will likely be criticism as you strive to make changes in your life. Some people may prefer you stay stuck in self-pity, lowered self-esteem, and lack of self-respect. It's a curious phenomenon that some individuals like to surround themselves with those who are in a low place, because they feel better about themselves in comparison. Instead of worrying what other people think or say, remain steadfast in your core beliefs and values. This will help you restore the self-respect you earnestly desire.

Work on changing your perceptions of yourself and others

In line with the recommendation to refrain from worry about what others think is the advice to change your self-perceptions and how you perceive others. Despite a fear that others are out to get you, or everyone else has it together except you, cultivate the more proactive perception that most people are good at heart and wish you well. Give yourself a pep talk, too, so that you encourage your own efforts at rebuilding and restoring your self-respect. After all, this is an integral part of overall well-being and living a life of purpose and joy.

Hold yourself to ambitious standards

While you may have done some dreadful things in the past, actions that caused you to suffer lower self-esteem, you can repair this damage by holding yourself to ambitious standards. Perhaps you lacked such standards before, so now is the time to embrace them. Never do something halfway or to the least of your ability. Pride yourself on following through on your word and mean what you say. Value honesty, challenging work, and commitment above all else. If you start with these, you will begin to learn how to respect yourself.

Believe in your choices once you make them

Vacillating and trying to second-guess your choices is not constructive. What is, however, is believing in the choices you make and exerting whatever effort is necessary to bring about the changes you seek.

Work hard and acknowledge your efforts

Along with the belief that you can build or rebuild self-respect and holding yourself to higher standards, it is also vital that you work hard and take the time to acknowledge the effort you've already put in. When you map out a project or undertake a task, having a plan of action helps you adhere to the work. It also allows you to see the minor successes you have along the way and shows you where you may need to adjust your plan to accommodate the latest ideas or take advantage of lessons learned in the case of setbacks.

Instead of trying to impress others, follow your heart and do what's right

If you maintain a constant goal of living in truth and according to your values and beliefs, you will find it easier to do the right thing. You won't be so tempted to try to impress others by doing things that are against what you know to be true or what means most to you. Feel your direction from within and take appropriate action.

Recognize that self-respect is a building process

Just as it takes a while to lose your self-respect, it also takes some time to regain or rebuild it. If you've never thought about self-respect, this is an excellent time to weigh the merits of respecting yourself and tailoring your life so that you hold yourself in the highest regard. What you most value is what you will pay attention to.

CHAPTER NINE

YOU ARE YOUR SOULMATE

What if manifesting your soulmate using the law of attraction began with you?

What if soulmate manifestation was easy?

What if you didn't have to wait?

If you're like most people, you want to manifest your soulmate because you think your soulmate will…

…make you feel complete…

…make you feel good enough…

…make you feel loved…

But how can anyone make you feel loved if you don't love yourself?

If you go around all day, berating yourself, going over your "failures" or "flaws", how can someone give you the love and care you want, the love and care you need to give yourself in order to feel good enough?

When you become your soulmate, you will find your soulmate.

Stop waiting, and wondering when he or she will manifest.

Start loving yourself and giving yourself everything you expect your soulmate to give you, all that loving, caring, kindness, and amazing feelings of being oh so good, worthy, accepted, and wanted, and then you will find your soulmate. He or she will appear in your life as a mirror of the person you are.

You have so much love inside of you that's just waiting to come out. Instead of waiting for someone else to love and adore you, look within and see how beautiful and special you are.

Remember you must connect with the power inside of you.

When you forget how wonderful you are, it's natural to give your power away and allow your relationship (or lack thereof) with someone else to define you.

If you were to meet your soulmate tomorrow, would you judge parts of them as good or bad?

Of course not! You would accept them for who they are. You would love them for their imperfections.

What if what makes you different is what makes you beautiful?

Start giving yourself the same compassion and love you would give your soulmate.

When you love and accept yourself as you are, you are able to receive love and acceptance from another. It's only when you know what it feels like to be loved and accepted that you are able to use the Law of Attraction to manifest those feelings from someone else.

Being whole and valuable to society doesn't begin when you FIND someone.

You are not less of a person if you are single. You don't need to spend all your time trying to find "the one."

Relationships can be filled with a lot of doubts and fears, a lot of ups and downs, and a lot of tears and heartbreak, if you're looking for someone else to complete you. That is a tremendous amount of expectation and pressure to place on someone!

Your relationship or marriage won't be successful simply because you found your soulmate. You won't be happy together just because you have a lot in common. Being in love doesn't guarantee happiness. Relationships still take work, and they have their good and bad moments.

Instead of spending your time and energy looking for that special someone, become the person who can thrive in a relationship and make an amazing partner!

Focus on your own happiness and wholeness. Make your self-worth a priority. Know how to be complete, happy, and loved independently of a relationship or another person.

The more you do so, the easier it will be for you to attract higher quality partners who treat you well!

When you take responsibility for your happiness, and begin to love and accept yourself as you are, you naturally become attractive to others.

Become your soulmate and your soulmate will find you.

You are the only person with whom you will spend your entire lifetime. You are the only person who will be with you every moment of every day – past, present, and future.

Forgiveness: The Critical Law of Attraction Step

So many amazing, wonderful, kind, generous people beaten themselves up daily for failing to meet a self-imposed standard or a requirement someone else believes they didn't meet.

There are fantastic mothers and fathers beating themselves up for not spending enough time with their children, even though they were doing the best they could.

There are great men and women beating themselves up for not getting married by a certain age. They want to find the perfect person for them, and are actively looking. They don't want to get married just to get married. They are doing what is best for them, yet it haunts them.

So, I want you to ask yourself two questions:

1. What do you most regret about the past year?
2. What will you do about it this year?

Letting Go of Regrets

Whatever you regret, it's okay! You're human, and everyone makes mistakes. Everyone fails at something, has a goal they didn't meet. It doesn't mean you're a failure. It means you're normal!

I want you to understand that, and you did nothing wrong. You did the best you could at the time.

What are you going to do about it?

You're going to forgive yourself! I encourage you to take the biggest dose of forgiveness possible. Forget about what happened. Release it.

That's why you're not going to keep beating yourself up. You're not going to keep talking and thinking about everything that isn't right or what went wrong.

Negative thinking and self-judgment won't help you! They only attract more problems and lower your self-esteem, making you feel even worse!

Break the cycle!

Start fresh with forgiveness!

Write down everything you regret doing in the past. Forgive yourself for all of it.

I know it may be hard. But if you want to move on and create your best life, you have to forgive yourself.

Lack of forgiveness distorts the world around you. It's baggage filled with regrets and negative emotions. It's the lower vibrational energy and resistance that prevents you from manifesting your desires.

When you forgive yourself, you leave all of that behind. You shift the blocked energy that was created by regrets, blame, guilt, and shame. You raise your vibrational energy and attract better circumstances in your life.

Forgiveness is a way out of the past. It empowers you and frees you.

When you forgive yourself, you open yourself up to love. Heart energy flows freely. And magic begins to happen…

Abundance begins to flow in all areas.

Major shifts and transformations can happen quite quickly in the area you forgave yourself.

Your entire energy field changes as you are more loving towards yourself, allowing more loving circumstances to appear in your life.

Commit to forgiveness and watch the Law of Attraction change your life.

CONCLUSION

"Why is self-love important?" you might ask. For many of us, self-love might sound like a luxury rather than a necessity, or a new-age fad for those with too much time on their hands.

Ironically, however, self-care and -compassion might actually be needed most by those of us who work too hard and who are constantly striving to surpass ourselves and grasp the shape-shifting phantasm of perfection.

Most of the time, when we're being too hard on ourselves, we do it because we're driven by a desire to excel and do everything right, all the time. It entails a lot of self-criticisms, and that persecutory inner voice which constantly tells us how we could've done things better is a hallmark of perfectionism.

Studies have shown that perfectionists are at a higher risk of several illnesses, both physical and mental, and that self-compassion might free us from its grip. Therefore, perfectionism and self-compassion are inextricably linked.

Work to dial down the former and boost the latter, with the conviction that doing so will help you to lead a happier, more fulfilled life.

The ills of perfectionism

Most of us in the Western world have been raised to believe that perfectionism is a great quality to have. After all, being obsessed with perfect details leads to perfect work, and this personality trait gives us the opportunity to humblebrag during job interviews.

In reality, however, perfectionism is bad for you. Not just "not ideal" or "harmful when excessive," but actively bad. Like cigarettes or obesity.

A shorter lifespan, irritable bowel syndrome, fibromyalgia, eating disorders, depression, and suicidal tendencies are only a few of the adverse health effects that have been linked with perfectionism.

Recovering from heart disease or cancer is also harder for perfectionists, with this trait making survivors, as well as the general population, more prone to anxiety and depression.

Moving away from perfectionism

So what can we do to move away from perfectionism? First off, acknowledge that it's bad for you; beating yourself up over every little error gradually chips away at your sense of self-worth and makes you less happy. And you deserve better than this.

Find a quiet room with a mirror. Look at your reflection and repeat the following prayer five **(5)** times daily.

PERSONAL APOLOGY PRAYER

1. Repent- **I am sorry that I**

   _____

2. Forgive- **Please forgive me for**

   _____

3. Gratitude- **Thank you for**

   _____

4. Love- **I love you for**

   _____

Fill in the blanks with something you can find within yourself to repent, forgive, show gratitude, and love inside of you.

Be truthful and find genuine expressions of the above.

Do this to remove the negative talk stored deep in your subconscious.

You are deserving and worthy. Always.

ABOUT THE AUTHOR

D.M. Woodard is a SAG-AFTRA and Actors Equity actor, flutist, and author of the new self-help publication, "When Your Soulmate Is -YOU: A Guide to Falling In Love With Who You Are." Woodard, a former Medical Assisting Instructor, writes about personal development and overcoming obstacles. Currently, she is in the process of writing a screenplay about Autism, a neurological and biochemical disorder she fiercely advocates and is personally affected by as a proud mother of an autistic daughter.

D.M. Woodard's debut instructional book guides you to the process of finding true love, starting with one's self. She explores ways to fall in love with yourself without embarking on narcissism, but internal love. She includes the Law of Attraction and the Hawaiian Self Prayer, Ho'oponopono principles, to plant seeds of change in the subconscious.

Woodard is an alchemist and student of the Law of Attraction. She has studied hidden sciences as well as other spiritual practices. She is currently working on obtaining her BFA in Theatre Performance and Studies from the University of Maryland, Baltimore County, and has taken creative writing courses. Further, she is a staunch supporter of environment conservation, and Woodard has the title of "Lady of Glencoe, Scotland."

D.M. Woodard desires that this book inspires and propels the reader to find the greatness and love within themselves.

REFERENCES

www.simplifyinginterfaces.com "*95 percent of brain activity is beyond our conscious awareness*" August 1, 2008 Marc Van Rymenant

www.link.springer.com "*Effects of Group Practice of the Transcendental Meditation Program on Preventing Violent Crime in Washington, D.C.: Results of the National Demonstrations Project, June--July 1993*" John S. Hagelin, Maxwell V. Rainforth [...} David W. Orme-Johnson June, 1999

"*The Hidden Messages in Water*" Masaru Emoto September, 2005

www.frontiersin.org "*The Easy Part of the Hard Problem: A Resonance Theory of Consciousness*" Tam Hunt and Jonathan W. Schooler   2019

"*Sync: How Order Emerges from Chaos In the Universe, Nature and Daily Life*" Steven Strogatz   November 3, 2008

WHEN YOUR SOULMATE IS - YOU

www.ingramcontent.com/pod-product-compliance
Lightning Source LLC
Chambersburg PA
CBHW071518040426
42444CB00008B/1706